DR. STACEY EADIE

# *Maternal* INSTINCT

## RAISING BLACK SONS TO THRIVE

# Contents

# Dedication

Dedicated to Sadiq Ali Martin, Kenneth Blake Bowman,

and Bruce Hamilton—Black sons whose lives were taken prematurely.

Much obliged to my loving husband, Phene Jean-Claude, and children, Phene Laurent and Xay. Thank you for your understanding of the time spent for the sacrifice of writing this book.

# Foreword

*My mother: Stacey Eadie Jean-Claude …*

Those of you who know my mother know her as driven: she is a pediatrician, wife, mother, friend, confidante, avid/die hard New Edition fan, woman of Alpha Kappa Alpha Sorority, Incorporated, and is now starring in her newest role as author. And yes, while I know and love her and understand her to be in these roles as well, one of the ways that she has shown her continued commitment to me, and my success, is in the role of driver. In my soon to be 20 years on this earth, my mother has been the driver (literally and figuratively) of my journey towards becoming a successful and grounded Black male. This success spans academics, my spiritual upbringing, and my emotional stability with personal growth and development.

My mother made sure education was a priority for me. My early childhood memories include being in the car with my mother and her driving me 45 minutes one-way to school while songs like "Boys to Men" by New Edition were playing in the background. So, am I saying that no other school was closer than 45 minutes away from our home? No, our district school was right outside of our neighborhood. However, after due diligence and research, my mother discovered that the academics were not as good at this school and would not have been as challenging for me. Subsequently, she made the time commitment to drive me to school 45 minutes away for elementary school and middle school despite her own medical practice being in the opposite direction. After she dropped me off at school, she would head back in the direction of our home and drive past it another 15–20 minutes to get to the area of town where her practice was located. From 1st grade through 8th grade, this was the commute for my mother and me. It paid off in huge returns when I was accepted to a Magnet Program at a Blue Ribbon High School, which also had the benefits of being a 10 minute drive from our home and I could ride the school bus to school.

As a young child, I did have a sense of understanding why I was not attending neighborhood schools that were not as academically challenging or had more distractions. My mother did not want me getting caught up in those distractions and wanted better opportunities. In the schools that I attended, I was able to surround myself with other academically focused kids and learn from them. I have been able to set goals and plan for myself with plenty of self-preparation beforehand. I have earned plenty of A's in school but have also failed in efforts as well. The impact of being in an environment with others who have the same mindset as me is not limited to the academic arena; there are also social–emotional influences. I have learned that I am going to make mistakes, but as long as I learn something from the mistake(s), the experience will not be a loss. If I were able to speak to my younger self, I would remind myself to take time and make mistakes and try new things. There is no hurt in finding out that you don't like something.

Long commutes with my mother extended beyond school for me and did not stop after 8th grade. I have been going to the same church for over 18 years and our church home is also 45 minutes away, located in yet another part of town from our home. As a member of our church, I have been involved in many activities and programs throughout the church including being on the Usher Board.

We attend church most Sundays and revive our spirit under the guidance and influence of our pastor, who is a Black male. I respect and admire our pastor; I see a lot of qualities in him that I see or want to see in myself. As a college student, I have Bible Study with my college mates, even those from different religions and backgrounds. At times, religion may have seemed like a chore, but not so much anymore. I understand the Bible so much more and am even able to talk to my peers about it. Staying close to God is a priority in my life. Reassuring myself through Word and prayer keeps me motivated even when challenges or unwelcomed situations arise in my life.

There is a parallel between my life and my parent's that I see when I consider the extended network of Black men that are in my life. First and foremost, I have my father as an example when I think of his childhood friends and his fraternity brothers. My father came to this country from Haiti when he was 13. His American childhood friends welcomed him and even helped him to perfect his English. They are close to this day, 30+ years later. In college, my father had the opportunity to have a newfound type of brotherhood when he became a member of Omega Psi Phi Fraternity, Incorporated. In their commitment to community service, I have seen my father participate

As a Black male in this society, I have had my fair share of encounters with social injustices that have also occurred against previous generations. Despite my mother strategically placing me in environments where I have been able to grow and push myself more, she still has had to have "The Talk" with me about being pulled over by a cop and conversations about the ways to deal with police. Learning to calm down, not get riled up, and not giving a reason through speech or deed to escalate has gotten me through these types of difficult situations.

in year-round activities and have even had the chance to join him and his fraternity brothers in feeding the homeless for Thanksgiving in West Baltimore.

On a peer-to-peer level, two of my closest friends and I have been at school together throughout our K–12 academic careers. The three of us have continued on the same path to college. However, two of my closest family members, who were like my big brothers, had a series of events that shook my world. One is no longer here because he was murdered shortly after his high school graduation. He did not plan to go to college; he was interested in starting his own business and my mother was helping him to figure out exactly what he wanted to do and how to become an entrepreneur. My other family member made a decision in his late teens that left him incarcerated and we lost six years of time together. The time that has been lost is irreplaceable, but I am proud of him and how he has overcome this adversity to move forward in a positive direction in his life.

If I did not have the mother I have, I would not have been

 exposed to the various opportunities and experiences I have had. I would not have learned to be so loving with friendships and to go the extra miles for those friends. The love and support I give has been returned to me 100-fold, and I am grateful for my family and friends.

The foundation my mother provided for me is indispensable and invaluable. All of this, and more, is what gave me a sense that I could achieve success in life and set and achieve goals that may seem unimaginable. There is a special bond between my mother and me. Her impact on my life as I transitioned from a boy to a young man is immeasurable. *Maternal Instinct* is her prescription of what it takes to raise a Black son to thrive. I completely agree with her take, as I live through the influence of her approach. I am proud to be called the son of such a phenomenal woman. My hope is that you too connect with a nugget or two that inspires you to follow your own path to *Maternal Instinct.*

# INTRODUCTION

*"But surely to tell these tall tales and others like them would be to spread the myth, the wicked lie, that the past is always tense and the future, perfect."*

- Zadie Smith

Early in history, society at large perceived a need to fear the presence of Black boys long before they could experience mature development. Tamir Rice and Trayvon Martin are two of too many young lives taken as evidence of dark and evil perceptions. However, self-imposed fears of sons of color date back long before modern day atrocities. Mothers of sons of color have endured trauma since they first witnessed their sons snatched from their breasts in African villages and during the slave auctions in America and Europe. These mothers were left feeling powerless to protect and control their sons' destinies. Post-traumatic stress caused an over-vigilant concern for the well-being of sons and their futures. Even a lioness fears her cub's prey. This instinctive nature caused reflexive responses of survival and protection. This is *Maternal Instinct*. It is an innate response or reaction to events or ideology that either poses a threat or brings pleasure.

The relationship between Black mothers and sons is a complex and multifaceted one, shaped by various historical, social, cultural, and political factors. From slavery and Jim Crow segregation to contemporary issues of police brutality and mass incarceration, Black mothers and sons have faced unique challenges and experiences

1

that have both strengthened and strained their relationships. Black mothers have nurtured, protected, and advocated for their sons. They have forged against systemic barriers and violence to confront evils that loom at the opportunity to devour a kingship.

**The transatlantic slave trade and enslavement**

The history of Black mothers and sons in America begins with the transatlantic slave trade, which saw millions of Africans forcibly taken from their homes and brought to the Americas to work as slaves. During this time, black mothers were routinely separated from their children, sold off to different slave owners, and subjected to brutal violence and exploitation.

Despite these challenges, Black mothers still found ways to protect and care for their sons. They often employed strategies of resistance, such as teaching their sons how to read and write or passing down traditions and cultural practices. Black mothers also used their position as caretakers to instill values of strength, resilience, and dignity in their sons, despite the harsh realities of slavery.

During slavery, Black mothers and sons faced the constant threat of violence and exploitation at the hands of their slave masters. Slave owners often used black men as breeding stock, impregnating Black women in order to create more slaves. This led to a breakdown in traditional family structures, with black men and women often having children with multiple partners.

Despite these challenges, black mothers still found ways to protect their sons from the worst of slavery's brutality. They often taught their sons how to navigate the dangerous terrain of plantation life, advising them on how to avoid confrontations with white overseers or how to hide from slave catchers.

**Reconstruction and Jim Crow Segregation**

Following the Civil War, Black mothers and sons faced new challenges as they sought to build new lives in the aftermath of slavery. During this time, many Black families were torn apart by poverty, violence, and discrimination, as they struggled to find work and secure basic necessities like food and shelter.

Black mothers often played a central role in the survival and well-being of their families during this time. They worked long hours in low-wage jobs, often with little or no support from their male partners, to provide for their children. Black mothers also served as moral and emotional anchors, helping their sons navigate the difficulties of growing up in a society that viewed them as inferior.

Despite their resilience, Black mothers and sons faced significant challenges during the era of Jim Crow segregation. The violence and discrimination that characterized this time were particularly harsh for black men and boys, who were often targeted by white vigilantes and police officers.

Black mothers found themselves in the difficult position of trying to protect their sons from the worst of this violence while also preparing them for the realities of life in a racist society. They often had to teach their sons how to interact with white authority figures to avoid confrontations or physical harm.

**The Civil Rights Movement and beyond**

During the Civil Rights Movement of the 1950s and 60s, Black mothers and sons played a crucial role in the fight for racial justice and equality. Many Black women and children participated in protests, marches, and other acts of civil disobedience, often putting themselves in harm's way in order to challenge the status quo.

Black mothers and sons also played a central role in the development of Black Power and other movements of the 1960s and 70s. These movements sought to challenge white supremacy and systemic racism in all its forms, and often emphasized the importance of Black self-determination and community empowerment.

The relationship between Black mothers and sons during this time was shaped by both the opportunities and challenges of the Civil Rights and Black Power Movements. On the one hand, these movements offered a sense of hope and possibility for black families, as they sought to challenge the injustices of segregation, discrimination, and police brutality. On the other hand, the movements also exposed Black families to new forms of violence and oppression, as they faced increased surveillance, harassment, and state repression. Black mothers and sons were often at the forefront of these struggles and faced a range of challenges as they sought to navigate the complexities of the movement.

One of the most significant challenges facing Black mothers and sons during this time was the threat of state violence. Police brutality and other forms of state-sanctioned violence were common during the Civil Rights era, and many Black families were targeted by police officers and other law enforcement officials.

Black mothers often found themselves in the difficult position of trying to protect their sons from these forms of violence while also encouraging them to participate in the movement. They had to balance the desire to empower their sons with the need to keep them safe, and often had to make difficult decisions about when and how to involve their children in the struggle. Despite these challenges, Black mothers and sons continued to play a central role in the Civil Rights and Black Power Movements. They organized protests, participated in boycotts and sit-ins, and fought for the right to vote and access to basic services like education and healthcare. In doing so, they helped to transform American society and pave the way for future generations of Black activists and leaders. Their efforts also helped to forge a powerful bond between Black mothers and sons, as they worked together to challenge the forces of racism and oppression. The movements exposed the deep-rooted inequalities and injustices of American society and highlighted the ongoing struggle for racial justice and equality.

Black mothers and sons have continued to face a range of challenges in the years since the Civil Rights Era. Police brutality, mass incarceration, and other forms of systemic racism continue to impact Black families, and many mothers are forced to navigate the complexities of raising sons in a society that too often sees them as threats. Black mothers and sons have remained resilient and determined, drawing strength from their shared history of struggle and resistance. They have continued to advocate for their rights, demand justice and equality, and work to build a better future for themselves and their communities.

## Maternal instinct awareness

My initial awareness of maternal instinct blossomed after learning that my husband and I had conceived a son. I dreamed of having a son as my first child since my parents' firstborn was also a son; however, I had not thought of the potential obstacles he would have to bear. I would have to allow him to get wiser through growing pains and not shield him from mistakes. I would even have to witness his mistreatment, confirming his witness at a tender age that he was dealt a card that would not give privilege to a less complicated path, or reward as his Caucasian counterparts. Thus, I had the same fears as my great-great-great-grandmother. This was not a conversation passed through generations.

I wondered why my mother and other matriarchs in my family never spoke of this concern or fear. I cannot recall ever overhearing conversations about this subject. It was apparent that these women had a special bond with their sons and protected them. Perhaps they kept it hidden to guard their sons' vulnerability, or perhaps they handled it in the same way they handled other challenges: by giving support and love until the next obstacle came along, but silently suffering. But maybe if it were spoken about, I would have been better prepared to face the many challenges and fears I would face raising my own son. Or, maybe my feelings of fear and isolation would at least have been lessened.

Initially, I did not feel any anxiety from my husband, nor did I feel any sense of urgency from him to make a disaster plan for how we should raise our son. Then, as I was exposed to more mothers at sporting events, through school, on social media groups, and through conversations at my office, I heard subtle comments that led to introspection. Without using words, our eyes would connect, and relief and trust allowed us to acknowledge something intangible but real and mutual. I connected with the feeling they were having and the experiences they might have seen their sons go through. The more I connected with them, the more I peeled layers to find out what these moms were feeling. As we talked, at times with tearful eyes to affirm that I understood, I revealed that I also have a son and told them, "I know what you mean." A reassuring and therapeutic feeling of catharsis emerged in that moment of safe space. These conversations were the beginning of my healing and eventually led to the end of my feelings of isolation and loneliness. I experienced the effects of hundreds of years of an enslaved mind, free but fearful.

Opening Pandora's box to talk about the fears of raising Black sons can be scary. Do we feel paralyzed or just alone? Society has buried its dark secrets and dares one to speak about its evil institutional traditions. For many, the solution is to make an example of the taboo myths of injustice that are now caught on video. While on the other hand, predators give self-serving stories of being the victim when they are exposed, such as in Trayvon Martin's "murder." They then justify their actions based on rules they manipulate to receive empathy from those who refuse to oppose them. Ownership would validate and awaken a conscious acknowledgment of the truth of their ancestors' guilt and their very own hidden racist acts. So, they ignore, distract, belittle, counterattack, and disconnect to veil injustice.

With the increase in global violence and racial and social integration, the need for this discussion with mothers of sons of color is critical. This book is a starting point for talking with not only mothers of color, but for extended family and guardians of all ethnicities raising males of color or any resemblance. This includes the mother migrating from another country who has plans of moving with her son, or thinking of sending her son with family members who live in a racially biased society. If you are a female planning to marry a male of color, this book will hopefully give you some insight to better understand the role of your partner's mother in his life and better prepare you for raising your son of color. This book can benefit teachers, civil service workers, physicians and persons interested in sociology. Understanding the culture of others and acknowledging the intentional oppressive role of a society that shaped some of its social behaviors are the keys to eradicating the need for this book. In Part II of this book, I share strategies that can serve as a practical guide to ensuring the success of our sons, grandsons, students, and neighbors of color.

**Who is considered a male of color?**

A male of color is any male who immediately may be excluded from the White population due to melanin or features not typical of White Europeans. Influenced by the media, society has depicted males of color as untrustworthy, uneducated, ignorant, or lazy "thugs." This terrorist plan was reinforced in movies like *Birth of a*

*Nation* when Black men were depicted committing violent acts against White women to create fear and make it easier to persecute Black men. Unfortunately, people of color are now following Hollywood's demand to play roles in movies and on reality TV that further stereotype Black men and women.

In American society, males of color are commonly judged prior to judicial review, often by citizens without credentials or an understanding of due process. Caucasians are increasingly using emergency services to report non-emergency civil complaints against African Americans. Such complaints are often made to have the African American in question arrested—however, the sentence could, in fact, be fatal. This is becoming a common topic of heated discussions because we have witnessed unwarranted deaths. Irresponsible citizens and corporations need to be held accountable and made to face the law for humiliation and defamation of character. Our mission should never be to prove we are worthy of respect because respect is a human right, nor should our goal be to step on the backs of others in the same barrel. Self-respect should be the ultimate achievement in life. The goal should be to hold society responsible for its biases. We must respect, protect, and empower one another to elevate ourselves. We need clean-cut rules that provide justice for everyone. The reality is that most times, your son will not be judged while behind your protective shield. His vulnerability will belong to the moral judgment of persons who make quick assessments that could be critical in matters of survival.

The worldview of Black lives has been devalued. It seems as

if the preservation of wild animals is of more priority than that of Black lives. I recall listening to a conversation on a national news show discussing the need to save koala bears in Australia. The sense of urgency and compassion expressed by the reporter persuaded viewers to join the efforts of organizations through donations and voluntary efforts. Significant airtime was given to organizations teaming together to save wild species despite the violence and resistance toward humans. I wondered why the same level of empathy was not given to human beings. Black males' extinction is the result of centuries of oppressive systems reminding him that no one is here to save him. Could people be so heartless as to turn a blind eye to the destruction of one lineage of males? Is your mindset that they are not worthy? If so, you should ask yourself, "Is the koala more worthy of protection than Black males?" Rescuing animals but not humans is unethical and immoral. The imagery of this plight played out for Black males by our society is matched with heartless comments of his self-deserving sentencing when his life is taken, or opportunity denied. Despite all the elements constantly tearing away at his efforts to survive, few find the possible threat of his extinction worth preventing. There is little echo of mercy or regret.

The innocent lives of so many victims have been snatched. Some are known to all the world, but others are known only to their communities and loved ones. Some lives were taken by police and others by citizens. Some were left alive with life-long scars and trauma, while others were taken too soon, families were fractured and are left to mourn. To keep their names and memories alive, I name some of them here: Sadiq Martin, Kenneth Bowman, Bruce Hamilton, Rodney King, Abner Loima, Amadou Diallo, Sean Bell, Oscar Grant III, Trayvon Martin, Eric Garner, Michael Brown, Laquan McDonald, Akai Gurley, Tamir Rice, Walter Scott, Freddie Gray, Sandra Bland, Samuel DuBose, Alton Sterling, Philando Castile, Korryn Gaines, Terence Crutcher, Stephon Clark, Bothan Jean, Javier Ambler, Ahmaud Arbery, Breonna Taylor, George Floyd, Rayshard Brooks, Daunte Wright, Andre Hill, Manuel Ellis, Tyre Nichols, and Jordan Neely.

**Changing the narrative**

It is time that an ethical and moral statute be in place to protect Black males as an endangered species. I'm talking about a concrete policy with funding to declare the country will protect each precious life. This is a type of reparation that acknowledges centuries of torment and suffering. Millions of tax dollars have been abused to support negligence and excessive police force. These resources could be channeled into education, recreation, medical care, and nutrition to help our youth thrive.

As a pediatrician for over twenty years, I have experience in maintaining the health of thousands of children. Part of my approach to helping families is to educate parents to recognize important developmental stages, diagnosis and best treatment practices for medical illnesses. I am on a mission to empower parents to advocate for the needs of their children. I have an acuity for understanding the external influences that may affect the lives of the children in my care. My *Maternal Instinct* gives me a practical advantage. It also allows for compassion toward all my families, understanding the pressures and demands of parenting.

11

In this book, I offer my professional and practical experiences to lay a foundation and propose growth strategies for the earlier phases of a Black son's life experience. I share reflections of the history of a mother-child relationship and then I discuss my personal encounters to set the stage for the origin of my fears. Lastly, using my own experiences, I focus on five areas I believe make a difference when raising Black boys. The areas include brotherhood, injustice, education, economic empowerment, and extracurricular activities. What I share is not conclusive or exhaustive considering the many threads of topics that need to be addressed in raising thriving Black sons. This is merely an attempt to open the door for conversations that honor an exchange of ideas that align to support and assure the success of Black boys, individually and collectively.

In advance, thank you for your support of this project and in the uplifting of Black boys everywhere. My hope is that your dedication and our collective instincts ignite a movement of love and protection.

# PART I
# PERSPECTIVES

*"You can't separate peace from freedom because*

*no one can be at peace unless he has his freedom."*

*- Malcolm X*

# Chapter 1

## Mother and Son

*"To know how much there is to know is the beginning of learning to live."*

-Dorothy West

The Willie Lynch Letter is a supposed speech that was allegedly given by a British slave owner named Willie Lynch in 1712, in which he outlined a strategy for controlling and dividing African slaves by pitting them against each other based on their skin color, physical characteristics, and other factors.

However, there is significant debate among historians and scholars about the authenticity of the letter. Many believe that it is a fabrication created in the 20th century to perpetuate the myth of white superiority and justify racial inequality. Regardless of its origin, the letter has been widely circulated and has had a significant impact on discussions of race and racism in the United States. It continues to be a controversial topic.

The Willie Lynch Letter, whether real or not, contains passages that suggest a deliberate strategy for instilling fear in Black mothers for their sons. The supposed letter argues that by separating Black men from their families, pitting them against each other, and making them compete for resources and the approval of their White masters, slave owners could create a system of control that would last for generations.

The letter suggests that by creating a sense of fear and mistrust among Black men, slave owners could ensure that they would not band together to resist their oppressors. The letter states, "We must also break the spirit of the (Black) male; we must make him docile and submissive...we must use his own instincts for his own good."

Black mothers were likely afraid for their sons because they knew that the slave system was inherently violent and brutal. They knew that their sons could be beaten, sold, or killed at any time, and that they had little recourse for protection or justice. The Willie Lynch Letter, whether authentic or not, played into these fears by suggesting that Black men were inherently violent and that they needed to be controlled through fear and intimidation.

Overall, the Willie Lynch Letter, whether real or not, represents a disturbing aspect of American history and a legacy of racism and oppression that continues to shape society today.

I can only imagine the mental effects placed on mothers to preserve the family unit when fathers were either sold or killed. This was the foundation of mothers offered as a symbol of strength in the African American family.

Lynch's goal was to reverse the role of the mother and father to weaken the structure of the slave family—that is, to destroy the male slave's image by making the female slave independent in hopes that she would teach her female and male children reversed roles. She would train her son to acquire physical strength but keep him mentally weak and interdependent. She would encourage and model interdependence for her daughter, reassuring her that this process would continue for generations to come. The slave master beat the father almost to the point of death in front of his wife, child, and other males, to instill fear but spare his life because he was an "investment" to breed.

Again, whether this theory is fictitious or not, over three hundred years have expired, but the scenarios still exist. Welfare systems insist that women may only benefit if there is no male presence in the home. Various institutional scenarios, such as unequal educational opportunities, a lack of job access, high-discipline experiences from grade school, and injustice and corruption, keep Black males from gaining their independence and serving as heads of African American families. Black families watch as police continue to murder African American males without prosecution. According to Mapping Police Violence, Black people are 2.9x more likely to be killed by police than white people in the US. The National Institute of Justice states that one in every nine Black men ages 20-34 are incarcerated. How do we preserve our families?

**Generational inequalities**

Many of the issues facing mothers of Black boys are not new, and in fact, they have been present for generations. Despite this, society has often overlooked or neglected these issues in a number of ways.

17

First, there has been a tendency to view these issues as isolated incidents rather than part of a larger pattern of systemic racism and inequality. This has led to a lack of recognition of the root causes of these issues, which are deeply embedded in our society and require systemic solutions.

Second, there has been a failure to prioritize the needs of marginalized communities, including Black families. This has been reflected in policies and practices that perpetuate inequality, such as unequal access to education and healthcare, and discriminatory policing practices.

Third, there has been a lack of representation and leadership from individuals and communities most affected by these issues. This has led to a lack of diversity in decision-making and policy-making, which can perpetuate systemic biases and inequalities.

Finally, there has been a reluctance to have honest and difficult conversations about race and racism in our society. This has led to a lack of understanding and empathy for the experiences of marginalized communities, and a failure to address the root causes of inequality.

Addressing these issues requires a collective effort from all members of society, including policymakers, community leaders, and individuals. It requires a willingness to recognize the ways in which we have neglected and perpetuated these issues in the past, and a commitment to working towards a more equitable and just future.

There are several difficult issues facing mothers of Black boys.

Here are a few examples:

- Racial Profiling: Black boys are more likely to be stopped, searched, and arrested by law enforcement compared to their White counterparts. This can lead to a sense of fear and unease for mothers who worry about their children's safety.

- Discrimination in Education: Black boys are more likely to be suspended or expelled from school compared to their White peers. This can result in a disrupted education and hinder their future prospects.

- Police Brutality: Mothers of Black boys worry about their children being subjected to police brutality or becoming victims of excessive use of force by law enforcement.

- Stereotyping and Bias: Stereotyping and bias can have a profound impact on Black boys, leading to reduced self-esteem and limited opportunities.

- Systemic Racism: Systemic racism, such as redlining and mass incarceration, disproportionately affects Black boys and their families, creating systemic disadvantages that can limit their opportunities and hinder their success.

- Lack of Access to Healthcare: Black boys often face barriers in accessing healthcare, such as lack of insurance or limited resources in their communities. This can lead to untreated health conditions and a lack of preventative care, which can have long-term consequences.

- Environmental Injustice: Black communities are often disproportionately exposed to environmental hazards such as pollution, which can have negative health impacts on residents, including children.

- Economic Inequality: Black families are more likely to live in poverty or face economic challenges, which can impact their access to resources and opportunities.

- Educational Disparities: Black boys may face disparities in access to quality education and resources, which can limit their opportunities and hinder their ability to succeed.

- Violence and Trauma: Black boys are more likely to experience violence and trauma in their communities, which can have a lasting impact on their mental and emotional wellbeing.

It's important to address these issues and work towards creating a more equitable and just society for all children and families, regardless of their race or ethnicity. These issues can have a lasting impact on the mental health and wellbeing of Black boys and their families, and it's important to work towards dismantling systemic racism and creating a more equitable society.

**Trauma repeats itself**

Going back to the slavery of our foremothers, moms must have been traumatized by separation from their children. My children have never been in a situation where I felt that helpless; however, the thought of them left unsupervised with a stranger is overbearing. Knowing what the slave master did to both women and men, slave parents must have suffered severe depression and anxiety from the uncontrollable thoughts of their rebellious, defenseless children (or their mild-mannered children) being taken away and left to pure fate. So, just as parents today prepare their Black sons to carry themselves when in the presence of police officers, Black slave parents must have coached their young children for the haunting expectation of separation or trauma caused by Caucasians. That mother's love, that maternal instinct from the motherland voyages, has survived to reach the souls of mothers today.

Young mothers of today experience trauma while watching African American males repeatedly lose their lives due to excessive police force-with little to no consequences. Not only are the police killings disturbing, but so are the comorbidity and mortality of violence, drugs, and genocide in Black communities. So are the systems that have left young Black males feeling hopeless with no sense of self-worth. As a result, they do not hesitate to take another brother's life because of the pain of the reality that no one has ever shown or told him otherwise.

Are our politicians and community leaders listening? Rebuild our neighborhoods, recreation centers, and inferior educational systems. If this does not turn around, it leaves its citizens feeling worthless and mothers helpless. Mothers are left with many questions: "How do I protect my son?" "How do I keep him safe when he seems to be threatened by everyone?" How do I ensure he has a bright future?"

"Who can I trust?" The police are supposed to protect us, but a few of them are the same "civil" service workers who are killing, robbing, and framing our sons. This brings up many more questions and concerns: "Could my son be the next victim?" "Whatever happened to Officer Friendly and Smokey Bear?" "Where are all the role models?" "No matter what I have done, it doesn't change anything because it seems the only common denominators are the tone of his skin and the texture of his hair." Mothers of sons of color of the twenty-first century are experiencing very similar stresses as the mothers of previous centuries.

**Eradicate fear**

*"Fear not, for I am with you; be not dismayed, for I am your God; I will strengthen you, I will help you, I will uphold you with my righteous right hand." Isaiah 41:10*

The first step to eradicating fear is raising awareness. If we begin conversations with our offspring, we can change the narrative. Offering ways to prepare our sons for success would open opportunities for them to compete in the world. I am opening up a discussion to the moms of today. My great-grandmothers, who were enslaved, did what they needed to do, and thus, I am here. My paternal grandmother lost two of her sons in the South, and I am unsure exactly why. In both cases my family has been haunted with the fact that we will never receive the exact story behind their murders. My father fled the South like many, sacrificing his remaining formal educational years to join the military in hopes of gaining opportunities and supporting his family back home. He served in

Germany and escaped racial oppression and degrading reminders as a result of his Black label.

However, sacrificing and fighting for his country meant little in the United States. And to think that almost one hundred years after my father's birth, I am still stressed over my son's experience. I am vigilant to assure that he has a chance to receive a superior education, fulfillment of lawful rights to casually live without being profiled as his male peers of other ethnicities experience and live without the constant reminder that his skin is the reason others consider him inferior, a threat, and shameful.

The second step to eradicating fear is to recognize our sons' vulnerabilities and approach them with a strategy that benefits them. These vulnerabilities could be the environment, learning challenges, behaviors, addictions, or emotional pain. Exposing our sons to things that may expand their growth and extinguish their limits can help them tap into their talents and interests, transform their self-destructive behaviors, diversify their life experiences, and remind them of our love and support of his dreams, and (whenever possible) invest in life-changing opportunities. We must lay the foundation and know that God will see them through for His glory.

After making the commitment to write this book for self-therapy, I realized it would benefit others and wrote it with the goal of sharing some of my own insights for raising a Black son who thrives. I have observed behaviors that are unique to mothers of sons of color. This does not encompass all mothers with sons of color, but it does relate to a noticeable amount of them. Often, mothers have some anxiety about their sons' health and development. This behavior has only been observed and is based on my opinion—it has not been researched. I would like to term it "brandishing." It is a mother's defense to protect her son from the harm caused by a society she has witnessed discriminate against, destroy, and kill Black males.

# Chapter 2

## Injustice

*"Not everything that is faced can be changed; but nothing can be changed until it is faced."*

-James Baldwin

To recognize the fears of Black mothers that have existed for centuries, you must understand the origin of a corrupt and unjust system. History reveals that African American males have been targets of injustice in American society from the time they were enslaved until the present day. When slaves were set free by the Emancipation Proclamation and Thirteenth Amendment, laws known as the "Black Code" were put in place to recycle the needed unwaged slave labor that once provided wealth and production to Southern business and plantation owners. Black Code laws were meant to confine the large population of once-enslaved Black men and use them as unwaged laborers. A clause of the Thirteenth Amendment states that "Neither slavery nor involuntary servitude, *except as a punishment for crime whereof the party shall have been duly convicted*, shall exist within the

United States, or any place subject to their jurisdiction." These laws allowed the incarceration of Black men in large numbers for extreme reasons that would not have been considered criminal if White males had committed the same act.

This stands true today as evidenced by the unequal sentencing of Black criminals compared to White criminals. The system continues to make laws that show a disparity in sentence time between White and Black citizens. Slaves built the South, and without this inhumane system, the South would never have flourished. The Thirteenth Amendment to the Constitution was adopted in all but a few states by 1865, which abolished slavery and involuntary servitude with the exception of punishments for crime.

In the late nineteenth century, Southern states leased predominantly Black state prisoners who were held for unjust sentences. Black prisoners labored without pay to work under conditions "worse than slavery." To ensure that the majority of prisoners labored were Black, they excluded White prisoners held for the most heinous crimes such as murder, arson, robbery, and perjury. These were crimes often committed by White citizens who instead were rewarded with residence in the penitentiary.

Due to the clause in the Thirteenth Amendment, prisoners could not be compensated for labor while incarcerated, and private prisons could profit from their free production. Present-day African American males are represented as the majority of the prison population, yet are not proportionately represented in society. Due to centuries of suppression to maintain Caucasian political dominance, especially since those incarcerated like slaves have no right to vote, Black power has vacillated.

Some do not agree with the idea that African American men are needed for the private prison economy and are accounted for from the time they are in kindergarten. Money is allotted for prison space instead of educational resources that would help their advancement. The system is multifaceted with codependent inequities in education, employment, wages, opportunities to receive loans for homes or businesses, and political representation.

African American boys are suspended at a rate of 12.9%, which is three and one-half times greater than other students in California's public schools, as reported by San Diego State and UCLA researchers. Those in grades K-3 are 5.6 times more likely to be suspended than students of other races. This means more time outside the classroom, which leaves gaps in education and decreased confidence, not to mention a negative stigma, ostracism, and depression, which result in more acting out. It is a negative cycle perpetuated by a system designed to suppress students based on the color of their skin.

African American males are also more likely than other students to experience harsh punishments. Most times, the staff are not equipped with solutions to redirect behavior. I have noticed that less-experienced Caucasian female teachers who are less culturally diverse seem to have difficulty relating to African American boys in the classroom. This seems to ring true even when, in fact, their behavior is no different than that of their classmates.

# *Maternal* INSTINCT

**It hits home**

I remember receiving an email explaining that my son was being "disrespectful" in class and asking that we speak with him. My husband and I were immediately disappointed and upset that our son would "disrespect" an adult. We did what most parents might do and gave him a lecture because, culturally, to African American parents, the word "disrespect" represents the ultimate offense.

When he was finally allowed to speak, he explained that one of the students in the class made a smart remark to him on his way to the tissue box. My son responded by telling him to be quiet. This exchange between the boys disrupted the class. When he attempted to explain what happened, the teacher scolded him, and the other child was empowered with the understanding that he could receive a pass. We asked to meet, and the teacher responded that it was nothing really bad and that she simply wanted us to know. We insisted that we meet because the urgency of a midday email including the word "disrespect" could not have been because of the story he gave us, nor could it be ignored.

Well, my son's account was correct. Until we spoke with the teacher, he had not been given the opportunity to explain what the other student said to him. He felt relieved because he had been scorned twice—once by the teacher and once by his parents— without any respect being given to his feelings and without justice. Needless to say, we used this as an opportunity to encourage him to not let his emotions lead him because it would not get him justice.

This matter did not require either of us to take hours out of

28

a workday, and should have been resolved after class in a simple conversation. But had this incident been written up using the word "disrespect" or other chosen words, the offense could have escalated, especially if word was passed on to the principal. For my son, clearing his reputation while also having the support of his parents and the relief of disappointment and exoneration of punishment was most important. This was especially true since, although the teacher said it was all right, he may have been flagged as disrespectful, and his character may have been tarnished.

Related to this incident, we must keep in mind the possibility of bias and a lack of cultural sensitivity in our society. Recognize that some parents and educators have biases that can play out when there are conflicts involving an African American child. This may encourage parents to want the child to be held to the highest degree of punishment if they have any conscious or unconscious bias against Black people.

**It happens all around us**

I have also witnessed this as a professional. Often, parents can explain an incident reported at school, in their neighborhood, or at home. The rage incited when they reveal that the child was of a race other than White, speaks to their agenda as if the child had perpetrated the act with premeditation because of his race. I have witnessed this most often when Black or Hispanic boys have been reported as aggressors. Sometimes, the "victims" have reported their inappropriate behavior and gladly accepted relief of punishment by their parents with the understanding of their parent's bias and capitalizing on it to get a pass. In some cases when the child is interviewed and the parent is asked not to interrupt, both children seem to play a role.

Several times, history has shown violent acts against Blacks by insecure supremacist Whites. Violence is often tied to unrealistic fear of the advancement of Blacks in politics, education, jobs, or finance. Many Whites were outraged after the Civil War and perceived that White men's lives were sacrificed to save the lives of Blacks. This fueled violence by the spread of propaganda playing on the ignorance and fear of Whites who focused on Blacks receiving wages and competing for opportunities meant for Whites only. In 1863, The New York Draft Riots were started by poor White Northerners who feared competition with Blacks for jobs. In turn,they attacked military and government officials and stole valuables from a Black orphanage before setting it on fire—the same was done to other Black businesses as well. The bombing of Black Wall Street is another senseless act meant to set Blacks back after they had built wealth and financial independence.

Amidst the COVID-19 pandemic of 2020, Portland protests broke out after the murder of George Floyd by knee compression to his neck by White police officer, Derek Chauvin. I watched a protest in which White people made up nine of the ten arson charges and damaged 75% of the property. The media suggested that the Black Lives Matter organization and other Black protestors were responsible.

The above are just a few examples of countless incidents where the Black economy and opportunities were targeted by destruction and where no justice was served, or reparations delivered. Terrorists escaped conviction, and the reputations of the wrongly accused were not exonerated. And, if that was not enough damage, all this has been followed by the injury of another Black male, Jacob Blake, who was left paralyzed from seven shots in his back. On a traffic stop, Officer Rusten Sheskey shot Blake while his three boys were in the back seat of their family vehicle.

This is not shocking in our world, where calling the police on African Americans has become a power tool for the powerless, racist in our society. The moniker "Karen" has been given to White racist women who use their privilege to seek empathy from authority figures to successfully carry out microaggressions and get their way. We witnessed Karen first as a fictional character in Birth of a Nation. Smartphones have unveiled the myth to be a reality—and if that isn't enough damage done, she uses these same tactics to pull on the heartstrings of her peers. Apparently, this is much easier to do than to confess and apologize for her intentional manipulation and often manic, dramatized tantrums. Unfortunately, when mixed with aggressive, egotistic, and biased police officers, this could be a cocktail for a death sentence, unnecessary force with charges, or plain stress and worsening health conditions from accumulative microaggressions. The antidote is truth, consequences, justice, and sentencing of time served until there is a genuine transformation with integration into and service for the Black community.

We also must educate our children about the demons of the internet. We must make them aware that there is no privacy once you place your information out there—you leave a footprint that builds a profile for you based on the data you enter, including your financial information, personal searches, and likes and dislikes. Worse yet, our society is moving toward replacing systems, including medical and—even worse—judicial systems, that use computer programs and robotics instead of humans. These programs may not consider cultural differences and may be written by culturally biased individuals who program questions based on associations between words. This will be our future injustice. We are leaving one unjust system to possibly walk into something worse. A programmed system will manipulate us to think and react however it wants. Technology and computers with no emotional attachment will engrave an infinite footprint of an inhumane judge of our character, image, livelihood, and potential fate of our dreams. Lord help us.

On the flipside, African American males are also committing genocide to their own existence. What would happen if this self-destructive behavior ceased? This would mean a stop to the selling of the drugs that continue the incarceration cycle and the slow death and destruction of family members due to drugs. It would lead to the demand that taxpayers' monies be used for the early education of youth, not prisons in which young men lose their freedom and are forced to work for no pay. We would no longer sell these citizens' freedom, nor would we accept the modern-day slavery made legal by a permanent, unamended law from the nineteenth century. In exchange, they would demand an education that produces a career, credit, and freedom. Communities would be cleaned up and rebuilt to instill a sense of pride. Resources would be included for stronger, more effective education systems and structured recreational facilities to foster proper development. Programs would be offered that give people tools to become more independent by teaching fundamentals such as financial investments, the importance of healthy living, the power of voting, and mental wellness.

African Americans of today are the seeds birthed from the ancestors of Black slaves. We have survived hundreds of years of sheer torment, racism, and the torture of each new trap produced to destroy our reason to live. The destructive schemes of the oppressor have caught up and crossed racial barriers. We must recognize our power and not weaken our existence.

The seed that brought you this far on this journey was made from an unbroken spirit of strength. We owe it to those who never quit because they had faith that if they endured a living death, we may rewrite the history of their dreams. African Americans were taken from Africa, brought to a country as a minority in a system where his purpose was to be a slave. He was separated from family under the most inhumane circumstances and then eventually set "free" with no resources or income to survive.

Meanwhile, the continuous development of systems and laws are constructed two steps ahead with the intent to oppress and continue the cycle. Until we have leaders in power with consciousness, lacking a mindset of self-wealth and immorality, pure justice is a fantasy. Think about it: every leader seeking pure justice was labeled a threat and taken out before they could overthrow the evil powers that worked decades in advance to keep the masses oppressed and blind. Our sons are at the bottom, struggling to breathe. What are we going to do moms?

# Chapter 3

## Her Story

*"For while the tale of how we suffer, and how we are delighted, and how we may triumph is never new, it always must be heard. There isn't any other tale to tell, it's the only light we've got in all this darkness."*

-James Baldwin

In the early 1970s, an infant was delivered at a local hospital in Baltimore, Maryland, before the years of routine fetal ultrasounds. Upon the child's delivery, the physician realized the infant had a rare fetal defect: her intestines herniated through the skin to the outside of her abdomen. Born with an omphalocele at a local hospital, I was separated from my mother and rushed to another hospital with surgeons experienced in correcting this defect. My father arrived, and the surgeons explained that my chances of survival were slim—only one out of eight infants survived the operation. After a successful surgery, I was discharged from the neonatal intensive care unit and sent home to my parents and big brother.

My family lived on a street with less than thirty single-family homes during a time where you left your doors unlocked and your neighbors were caring and watchful. My mother was a graduate of Bowie State University and was a successful special education teacher in the Baltimore City Public School System for years, back when the school system was open to teachers developing individualized plans to accommodate lessons for various learning styles.

During my early beginnings, Ms. Bertha kept me while my parents worked. This was when I learned to play jacks with her granddaughters, who were older than me. Rita, a light-complected preteen with beautiful long, wavy ponytails, was my favorite to play with. She was not diplomatic with her jacks game and gave no thought of cutting me any slack just because I was only four. As a treat, on some days, they would take me a few doors down to Mr. Smokey at the corner liquor store at Fulton and North Avenue to purchase my favorite chocolate Lance cookies with the vanilla filling. Being the youngest had its advantages, as Mr. Smokey would often slide me a pack when we were just there to make a run for Ms. Bertha.

Also, it was at my babysitter's home where I learned the craft of cursing that no other four-year-old could top. My aunt told me a story of when we visited her home, a mere mile away from Ms. Bertha's, and my brother ran to her in the house with me quickly on his heels, as he was tattling that I called him an "MF." Quick to my defense, I disputed his point, saying, "Na on, I called him a motherfucker." I have no recollection of those memories, of course.

My parents would have to clean up my act before enrolling me in a private Baptist preschool, Wayland, that was en route to my mother's job. I could not wait to enter kindergarten and travel across town to the elementary school where my mother taught and where my brother attended. My father had an entrepreneurial spirit. He owned an eighteen-wheeler rig, and he and my mom had started a trucking company. He would often make runs across the country and back to drop loads. When he returned, he would take my brother and me for rides and allow us to pull the loud horn. My favorite place was in the sleeper of the cab of the tractor-trailer. To this day, the smell of the soft leather bed mixed with exhaust fumes brings happy memories of my early childhood. I had a slight speech impediment, which may have been considered normal at my age. My father told me how I would tell people when asked that he was in "Bamalama" in his "fuck." I'm not sure if this was a part of the language I learned, but I also called my underwear my "foz."

We spent most of our time with close family or our church family. We were members of the Mount Hebron Baptist Church, where my mother was a secretary and sang in the choir, my father was an usher, and my brother and I sang in the young people's choir and played in the pews during service. Both my parents were active members of the Masonic Fraternity and the Order of Eastern Star. My father would line Masonic emblems perfectly along his bumper. I remember a gold ring with a red stone and the emblem in the center he wore faithfully on his finger. I knew it meant something significant but never asked. I observed his interactions with other brothers crossing the racial boundaries that were obvious in the '70s. He knew he could rely on his brothers when he needed to.

Eventually, I would enter the kindergarten class at James Mosher

# *Maternal* INSTINCT

Elementary School with my mother and brother. My kindergarten teacher was Mrs. Buckman, a sweet Caucasian lady whose classroom was filled with a child-size kitchen, dolls, and so many fun toys, but best of all, it was right down the hall from my mom's classroom. If ever she needed to send my mom a note, she would ask me to take it.

My mom taught what was known as special education for sixth graders, and I knew each of them. They really loved my mom, and most gave her a copy of their school pictures. During that year, my forty-one-year-old mother's health took a turn for the worse. My brother and I moved in with my great-aunt, Aunt Angie, for a few months. She lived a few blocks away from our elementary school, which meant we could finish the school year without disturbance.

I remember being dropped off. Aunt Angie had two older sons who would entertain us, which kept our minds distracted from our separation from what we had always known as home. When we returned home for the summer, my mom was frail and in a wheelchair. The once vivid and life-of-any-party woman was now solemn. She had been diagnosed with multiple myeloma with many extended admissions to the hospital for chemotherapy. We watched her body diminish into a frail frame, and she eventually succumbed to her illness after I turned six and before my brother's twelfth birthday.

**Transitions**

My father enrolled my brother and me in our home zone schools for the year. We adjusted quickly and made new friends. On the first day, my father drove me to school, introduced himself to my teacher, Ms. Cook, and told her about our family situation. He asked if she would mind checking my appearance and fixing anything that might be out of place—and to straighten me up and then call him if I stepped out of line. Ms. Cook looked up at him with an innocent smile and agreed. I dared not test his request, so I made every effort to be a good student. I could not recall my father ever spanking me.

To adjust to single parenthood, my father changed careers several times over a few short years in order to effectively parent two young children. His roles ranged from co-owner with my mother of a trucking company, employee of lumber company to haul lumber, a neighborhood variety store owner and finally working as a longshoreman at the Port of Baltimore. With unstable work hours posing a potential risk for safety, I moved in with my mother's sister, Aunt Ruby, who lived in Sandtown, in the middle of my second-grade year. I attended the elementary school where my aunt was a part-time crossing guard during the day; she also worked as a nurse at a nursing home that Aunt Angie managed. It was during this year that I discovered math was my strength. I was even invited to learn with the third-graders. My brother, who was six years older than me, was now in junior high school and continued to live at home with my father, who often worked late. Getting back to owning his own business, my father had opened a variety corner store where you could buy lunch meat, pickled onions, and a few other groceries. The store was in a neighborhood not far from where I stayed with my aunt.

Living in Sandtown was different for me. The houses were attached and had beautiful marble steps ("the stoop," we called it). After work and school, everyone in the neighborhood spent time together. The houses were close to the street, but we kids ran around and rode our bikes and big wheels along the sidewalk without harm. It was exciting, safe, and fun. Most of the neighbors socialized outside until sunset.

At the end of the school year, my dad came by to visit one afternoon, and I told him I was ready to move back home. With an astonished look on his face, he smiled, and that was when the next chapter of my life began. I moved back to our family home in Gwynn Oak with my father and brother. Living with my dad and brother was so pleasant. Our life was full of jokes, hugs, and the words "I love you." They were comedians who kept me from crying in seclusion over the loss of my mom.

When I turned nine, one of my close friends passed away. It was then that it really hit me for the first time that I would never see my mother again. Prior to my friend's passing, death did not feel permanent. Everyone would tell me I would see my mom again in heaven, but to my disappointment, it never happened and was not going to happen soon enough. It seemed as if I was losing everyone close to me.

My friend and I shared a special bond because we both were born with congenital defects—she had been born with a heart defect—and we had the scars of survival on our bodies. So, we did not feel so different when we were together. Most people asked if we were sisters, and we would smile mischievously and say yes. She lived near Aunt Angie, but one summer before she passed, my father allowed her to stay at our home for a week. There were not many kids on my block, but she and my neighbor had crushes on one another, so we planned a wedding and used the pom-poms from my shrubs as the bouquet. Looking back, I think how delightful it is that she was able to fulfill every girl's dream of having her wedding before leaving this earth.

I still have a memory of sitting in the pew at her funeral, looking up at the stained-glass windows and wondering why God would take the people I loved so much. How could he take a child with so much life? Could this happen to me as well? I, too, was born with a defect, and now I had no one to share that bond with. I knew no one else who had survived what we had survived and who made being different feel acceptable. I felt the need to find a way to stop sickness and keep babies and mommies living because they need each other.

**Family ties**

My father loved traveling to visit family. Several times a year, we visited his sisters and brother in Eadytown (Cross), South Carolina. It was an eight-hour trip by car, and we often traveled at night, possibly as part of my dad's plan to keep us from asking, "Are we there yet?" a million times. We always stopped at South of the Border, ate, and loaded up with fireworks for entertainment for all my cousins.

By the time we arrived on my family's forty-acre lot where most of my aunts, uncle, and cousins from South Carolina resided, the sun was awaiting its moment to rise. Whenever we turned onto the dirt road, my cousins were up and dressed and waiting; we had continuous fun, from the time the rooster crowed until it was pitch black (there were only a few lights off the road). My grandfather worked hard for pennies that he had invested in his real estate. He later sold part of it to a major corporation and willed the land to his children after his passing. As city children, my brother and I entertained ourselves by fishing, feeding my aunt's chickens and hogs, gathering eggs, hiking the hills for adventure, and visiting other members of my family. I have so many euphoric memories. It was a getaway from the fast pace of city life.

I was so impressed by my Aunt Maude's Cooking. I have never met a more experienced cook. She could take a package of chicken from the freezer and have it ready to eat in no more than forty minutes, and it was always seasoned perfectly and fell off the bone. She would also make vegetables and fresh beans with it, and she would never forget rice—Gullah Geechees never have dinner without rice. My family has a distinct heritage known to some as Gullah Geechee. They have a different dialect that attaches to you after a week or two, that you bring home with you, and that your friends question.

We could not leave South Carolina without traveling another two hours and spending a few days with my father's eldest sister (she was at least sixteen years older than my father) and her family. He loved his family, and, as he was their baby brother, they spoiled him in every way.

My father was the youngest and went off to the military at age sixteen in search of a better life. He wanted to be able to send money home to bless his family. He traveled the world and lived in Germany for several years. His mother passed away when he was in his young adult years, and his father passed not much later. My brother and I never met our dad's parents, but they left their legacy in the secrets of the land he was raised on and occasional reunions (which my children are now able to enjoy).

The remnants of the small, broken-down wooden building that my grandfather had built in the early 1900s were still standing when I was a child. It was used to hold the chicken feed. There was a large oak tree that was over a hundred years old and stood as tall as a two-story building. Its roots ran above the ground for several yards, which made it hard to ride our bikes. In the adjacent chicken coop, I would play with the baby chicks when they hatched until the rooster came along to peck at me and chase me away.

I would watch in amazement as my Aunt Maude managed the animals. She raised chickens, hogs, and cats. She spoke chicken—I swear they knew what she was saying to them and obeyed her every order. They helped each other. The rooster would crow in the morning at dawn, but she would already be awake cooking grits with either fish, bacon, or sausage. She would let the hens and rooster out and take a few brown eggs from the hens' nest with her to make breakfast. And before dusk, to protect them from the fox, she would call in a soprano octave, "Hey bitty bitty bitty bitty!" a few times, and they would come running from all over the land to feed inside the coop. These are my pleasant and sheltered memories of the South.

**Lessons from my father**

My father's childhood memories of South Carolina were of a very segregated racist majority. Because of these memories, he never tolerated anyone in his adult life treating him as anything less than a man. He served in the United States Army domestically and internationally in the 1940s. He ended his international travels and realized that while people in other countries treated him equally and with respect, racism was still Black people's worst enemy in the United States. He taught us self-pride and always built us up with praise and love. "I love you" were three common words in our home.

As my brother approached his teenage years, my father would often lecture him about how to conduct himself with his peers. My father bought him a brand-new car at sixteen. There were strict provisions for when, who, and where he could drive. And, of course, my father gave him the talk that every Black male is given before handing over the keys. The details may vary, but the purpose is to ensure a safe return home if pulled over by the police. My brother was told, "Keep your hands on the steering wheel—not too low, at about ten and two o'clock. Do not show off. Be respectful always. Get home, and I will take care of the rest."

I must say I was given this talk as well, with slightly different details. My father told me, "If it is dark, put your flashers on and slowly proceed to a well-lit intersection. Never stop alone on a dark road." When I lived in New York, he bought me one of the first cell phones ever produced and demanded that I call him as soon as I had been pulled over. We did not fully appreciate my father's wisdom until we matured, and we respect it even more now that we have children.

On Mother's Day and during summer break, my father drove us to the Eastern Shore of Maryland, to visit my mother's mother, uncles, and cousins, and we never forgot to visit my mother's gravesite. It was at this gravesite that I would witness my father weeping silently. I knew he must have missed her greatly. The challenge of raising two young children on his own was probably something he had never given a thought before her death. He fulfilled the roles of both mother and father with grace. During some summers to give him a break, I would spend a few weeks with my maternal grandmother. My uncles showed love by ordering my favorite crabs, fresh off the Chesapeake Bay. The taste of a Chesapeake Bay crab is ingrained in my memory for life.

I was the baby of a family with a generation gap, so I often had to use my imagination to play. I played in the yard, jumped the ditch, and ate blackberries—one time, I was met by a large black snake. The dragonflies taunted me in the yard, causing me to scream and run to my grandmother. My older cousins would often allow me to hang out with them.

Every year, our family had a traditional cookout with endless food. Also, when I was younger, there was a yearly bull roast held at the local Elk Lodge. Busloads of people would travel from New York, Philadelphia, Baltimore, and Delaware, including those who drove. There was music, an endless supply of food, and an adult lounge where they served alcohol. I was obsessed with the lounge because it was the only place forbidden to kids. They also had a DJ and dancing. Oh, if we could only get in. One year I ran in. It was dark with red and green lights flashing and loud music and smoke. I found my parents' legs before anyone could escort me out. After taking a few minutes to satisfy my curiosity, I was all better. Once I got back outside, my brother gave me a look that said *I told you not to go in*. I smiled back at him and enjoyed my time with the kids once again, dancing to and singing "Rock the Boat" and "Strawberry Letter 23."

I have never seen anything that could duplicate this type of entertainment. My mom's family knows how to party and enjoy life. My grandmother was the matriarch, and I learned so much from her, including a few of her baking and cooking skills. I was an expert at tasting the batter of her famous cakes—perfect every time. Her crab cakes were impeccable. Her sweet and loving spirit overflowed into her cooking. She and my Aunt Maude inspired my taste for good food.

**Competition**

During my later years of elementary school and middle school, I formed bonds with some of my male schoolmates. These guys were intelligent and competitive academically. They excelled without apology. I attended Roland Park Middle School, a diverse school whose students were selected from a pool of individuals recommended by elementary school principals across Baltimore City. As I recall, five students, mostly females, were selected from my elementary school. My Roland Park Middle School years were when I first experienced guys who were more competitive than my close girlfriends and me. I like to refer to them as brilliant. We established good relationships that would last a lifetime. An impression was forever stamped in my brain that boys could be distinguished and make it look effortless. Just to give an example of the talent this school attracted from the Baltimore metropolitan area, Tupac Shakur attended Roland Park—he was in my grade, although I never shared a class with him.

Upon graduating from Roland Park, I was accepted to attend Western High School, an all-female city-wide Baltimore public school and my first choice. I would no longer share classroom bonds with my male peers. This memory would soon vanish from my thoughts after being introduced to the many traditions of this historic institution for young women. I believe this crucial time I spent in the absence of males in the classroom may have erased my memory of previous experiences in the classroom and ignited my later fears of Black males' true zealous academic competitive nature. During high school, I would compete only with my female peers and understood the drive to excel from a female's perspective without any of the distractions or temptations that come with being in the presence of the opposite sex. I woke up each day and rushed to school to learn with my friends and hear our principal remind us of the expectations of a Western young lady on the morning announcements before first period: "Western Only the Best."

I visited several universities during my senior year of high school. My heart was set on attending a small university in Pennsylvania, approximately one-and-a-half hours away from my home. Lincoln University has a proud history of being the first historic Black university and a well-known stop on the underground railroad. Its graduates include Thurgood Marshall, Langston Hughes, Roscoe Lee Brown, Kwame Nkrumah, and Nnamdi Azikiwe. It was not hard to say yes to an offer for merit scholarship that included tuition, room and board, books, and stipend.

The program I enrolled in was called LASER (Lincoln Advanced Science Engineering Recruitment) and was funded by NASA. Before receiving the scholarship, all candidates had to successfully complete ten intense weeks—one-third the time of a usual semester—studying college courses such as Calculus I and II and Physics I and II.

Once again, I was able to experience studying with confident, competitive Black males. My awareness of the disparity in the ratio of males to females was heightened. I know this ratio did not represent true numbers of males with potential, and something must have happened during high school. When I returned home, I would often run into old acquaintances and get filled in on recent events in the neighborhood and my old schoolmates' lives. The stories were often disappointing. I remember perceiving that my male peers in my elementary and middle school years were pressured to meet the status quo and remain "cool" as they tried to balance being accepted by their male peers while keeping up with schoolwork. One wrong decision could change their fate. They could get involved in using or distributing drugs, not have proper recreation, and run into law enforcement, which often did not involve second chances or teaching moments.

During my sophomore year of college, I received a devastating call that my best friend's brother was shot and killed by the police. In 1991, my mind could not understand why a police officer would deliberately shoot into a vehicle and kill a high school student. As a child, I spent hours every day in their home and vice versa. This was trauma #1. I would experience a flooded consciousness of the invaluable fate of young Black males in society. Later, another schoolmate of mine was arrested for armed robbery at a fast-food chain. In college, other obstacles arise for young men who hope to avoid the law when traveling off-campus despite their educational status; my female counterparts and I did not have to encounter these obstacles on the same level. However, while on campus, these young men were able to be themselves, the naturally creative, talented, and competitive leaders they were born to be.

Lincoln University was a safe haven with plenty of opportunities and little institutional oppression and judgment to shame students for expressing themselves. It was here, under the leadership of two of my male colleagues—the student government president and vice president—that the students gained national attention for shutting the campus down until the president of the university heard our complaints that the security staff was incompetent. Outsiders visited the campus on weekends and harassed both male and female students with force. It escalated each weekend, and security tried but could not defuse the situation. A group of male students of the school stepped up during an attack from outsiders on a Friday evening to protect the student body after countless pleas to the university. A few students were injured by the invaders, but the culprits were captured (with a few injuries as well) and turned over to security. However, it was the students who were charged by local police, and these charges would hamper their future. In any other situation, they would be heroes, but not these Black males. There was no justice to prevail for their benevolence.

To achieve my ultimate destiny, I moved to New York to begin medical school at the New York College of Osteopathic Medicine. Here, I met academic challenges that exceeded any level of my education. Black males would not be counted out. I spent countless hours studying with these men—growing up in a household of men made it second nature. These men were brilliant, tenacious, and self-driven to achieve greatness. I know there are many more Black males that can achieve these levels of education.

The reality set in that the path to achieving my childhood dream did not include many faces that mirrored mine. To endure the rigor, I as a Black female would need to become one of only 2% of the physicians in America. Well, "We made it," we thought, just to face the grim reality that the systems we encounter throughout life have no ceiling or day of reckoning. We were now in a system that was not designed for all to succeed, a system of bell curves guaranteeing that 2.5% of students would fail each test. We were fighting against the current. While the majority were carefree, we would cringe from processing images of Black male genitalia displayed by professors to show the most severe cases of sexually transmitted diseases, which still play in my mind today. These subliminal yet deliberate teachings were very clear to each of us in our short white coats in the auditorium as we would catch each other's eyes across the auditorium and curl our lips to acknowledge the intent of this imagery to our White colleagues. However, this did not stop the Caucasian females from hitting on my brothers one bit.

For my Black male counterparts, the ratio of Black males to Black females in medicine is declining. There are many more Black males who can achieve these levels of education. All these memories of my education experience with Black males forged my determination that my son must be prepared to compete with his White counterparts. I also came to realize that an imperative tool for him to succeed was to ensure he learned the strategies of standardized test-taking because it was obvious my counterparts were taught this at a young age and had mastered it by graduate school.

**Fortitude**

My father's health declined while I was in medical school. This required me to travel home to Baltimore on many weekends to help make decisions related to my father's hospitalizations, discharges, and procedures. It would become unbearable and emotionally exhausting to concentrate on my studies. I opted to extend my time to ensure I finished and, more importantly, that I could be there for my only living parent, who had made so many sacrifices for me, including driving me out of state to all of my medical school interviews and assuring that I would make it to my destiny.

As my father's complications worsened, I found refuge in my pharmacology professor, Dr. Mancini, a stern-faced Italian man with broad shoulders. He was feared by most students because of his intimidating class and his tests with approximately 100 K-type questions. K-type questions are complex questions that give multiple combination choices for each answer. His class was so hard that the average score on tests was 50 percent. Often, a bell curve dictated which percentage of students failed and had to retake the exam. A few of the students in the class were pharmacy school graduates who struggled, which did not help the average (but was beneficial if you were close friends with these students and could study with them).

After confiding in Dr. Mancini about my father's condition—which was not easy because I usually kept my personal business to myself and did not want anyone to think I wanted sympathy—he would call me to ask about my father's medications and discuss other options for me to bring up with my dad's physician. He found so many interactions that caused other symptoms that are now tracked by databases. He was brilliant.

I was scheduled for my final test of medical school—I needed to pass to continue on to practice at hospitals. It could have all ended there. I had prepared for weeks by reading an entire book on the subject. At 11:00 p.m. the night before my test, my phone rang as I was sitting on the floor of my one-bedroom apartment in Queens, NY. I thought it was a very unusual time for someone to be calling. My heart started to flutter as it did every time my pager or phone rang, as it made me think of my father's complications. The first ring. *Should I answer?* The second ring. *No, I can't right now.* The third ring. *You have to. You can't just ignore it.* I picked it up. "Hello?" No one answered. Silence. "Hello?" I thought I heard a faint sound and some shuffling "Hel-lo."

Someone took the phone, and I heard my sister-in-law's voice on the other end. "Stacey," she said, followed by a brief silence. I could barely hear her weeping. "Stacey, he's gone."

I heard my brother's cries in the background. He attempted to speak to me but was unable to get any words out.

My sister-in-law said, "We're gonna call you back." I dropped my book, and all my life wanted to drain from me in an instant. I inhaled the fullest breath I could and released the strongest voiceless cry I had ever let out, followed by the ugliest cry ever.

In the chaos in my lonely bedroom, I heard my father's voice descending to the floor so clear that my cry stopped instantly. He said unfavorably, "Don't feel sorry for yourself." He often mentioned that in his teachings as I was growing up. He meant it with all his heart. The thought of self-pity disgusted him to the core.

"What?" I wondered aloud. "But isn't this the time for self-pity?" I was scolded in my grief. I washed my face. I picked up my book and sat back in my spot on the floor with confidence because I knew this was not only my dream but his as well. I quickly pondered, "Why tonight?" I studied for some time before curling up in my bed and crying myself to sleep. I woke up the next day and called my close colleagues, who begged me not to take the test. When I insisted, they called the school administrators, including Dr. Mancini, who was the advisor for the class. I drove into school with swollen blood-colored eyes concealed by the darkest sunglasses I could find.

Before I could enter the testing area, my advisor's assistant ran up to me and told me, "Dr. Mancini wants to see you immediately."

I walked into his office. "Kiddo," he said, addressing me by a nickname he had given me, "I can't let you go into this test. I have received several calls this morning and have heard your father passed last night. I am sorry for your loss."

I began to get tearful and said, "Yes, he did, but I have to take this test today."

"But do you understand if you do not pass this test today, your medical school career is over?"

"Yes, I do. I have been studying long and hard. I was able to get myself mentally together last night. I must go home to bury my father. I cannot keep this test over my head and peacefully make the arrangements for my dad."

"Ok, Kiddo." He gave me a hug and said, "Let's go in." I took my time reading every word of that test. When my mind would stray and my eyes would start to tear up, I remembered the words my father gave me the night before. I handed my test in, and everyone wished me a safe travel home. With my bags already packed, I anxiously hopped on the 95-south interstate to Maryland immediately after taking my test. I was relieved to be with my brother and the rest of my family within a few hours.

On our ride back after finalizing the arrangements with the cemetery, I received a call on my cell phone—which, back then, looked like a telephone receiver with a cord mounted into a NYNEX six-by-ten-inch imitation leather case that zipped up. There was no increased heart rate with this call. "Hello?" A familiar man's voice was on the other end. "My professor is calling me," I told my brother and sister-in-law. Now my heart rate increased.

"Hey, Kiddo, how is everything going?"

"I have peace."

"Well," he said before pausing for a moment. "I wanted to be the one to call you about your test."

My breathing stopped for a few seconds with splinting. "Yes?" I answered with despair.

"You did it. You passed the test."

I screamed out for the world to hear. "I passed the test!"

"I did not want you to have to wonder and wait until you returned. Now, complete your plans in peace. See you when you get back to start your clinical rotations. Congratulations!"

Now I understand. I had to know that God and my father were with me, which gave me major confidence. My favorite person on Earth had left, and I had to figure out how I would navigate life without him. I knew the extent of how blessed I was that God had given me a father who loved me with every morsel of his heart, had the work ethic of a thousand men, shared his wisdom to direct me in years unseen, honored family first by any means necessary, introduced me to God and led by his example, gave me a view of the sky on his shoulders, and challenged me as he was paving the foundation for me to achieve my dreams even in his absence. What a man! He taught me the importance of being the best parent you can be because you have enough love inside you to give for two parents, no matter your circumstance.

**Rock**

To sum it up, in most families, the parents have a significant influence on each child's life. My father raised two young children after losing his wife. He wore many hats—because of his determination to find the perfect balance between supplying needs for the family and being present for his children, he sampled careers as a truck driver, longshoreman, and entrepreneur of a store named Rock's Variety. Rock was the nickname his family had given him, but after we went south of the border, it was no longer just an alias.

I remember my father always mentoring young and older men, some of whom were relatives and others who were neighbors or friends. I learned most about my dad's influence and benevolence for others from these men themselves. I witnessed conversations my dad had with some of them. I pretended I was not there but absorbed his wisdom as a secondhand lesson. When family or acquaintances were in financial trouble, they would come to him. His words were not always diplomatic, but they were truthful, even if it tore your soul and ego apart. All knew he was genuine and never spoke with undertones of envy but always with sincerity, and so they listened. Some agreed, and others may have just accepted the words to get a reward. I did not always understand why they came to him with their situations when they knew what was coming to them. It was almost as if they needed someone authentic to talk to because he never cut anyone any slack.

His legacy is great because thirty years after his death, there is someone who reminds me of how much they miss him and what he meant to them. My favorite accounts are those that confirm his loyalty, stories of that guy who was there when no one else could be found. He helped others, but his life's purpose was to raise us, and he took great pride in his position. He carried a wallet full of pictures of us from our childhood through our high school graduations, and every conversation he had must have included us.

He was well-known in Baltimore, and as we rode through certain neighborhoods and someone recognized his car, there would be a short distinct beep exchange and maybe a "Hey, Eadie." When we walked through the grocery store, we stopped for conversations with people he had met somewhere. After a short exchange of sarcasm, jokes, and laughter distinct to men of his generation, they would say, "This must be your daughter that is going to be the doctor," or "Yes, she looks just like the pictures." I would get so embarrassed but would still smile. I knew it made him happy, so I would quickly get over it. They would inform me that my father was a "good man." That made me proud.

He was my sole advocate in ensuring I understood how important it was to dream and to see my dreams through. He would introduce me to every doctor I encountered as "my daughter, who plans to be a pediatrician." He purchased a real stethoscope so I could feel and listen to hearts like a doctor. And what doctor would not want a science lab kit to do their own experiments in? Well, I guess that fostered my major in chemistry in undergraduate school.

My father told his eight-year-old daughter, "You will become a doctor if that is what you desire." More importantly, he planted an entrepreneurial spirit within me and told me I could build my own office on the land we owned in South Carolina and take care of all the children there. This blew the ceiling off my eight-year-old mindset. I thought this man must have either been crazy or really believed in me. He thought this little girl born with a birth defect could accomplish that kind of dream. He broke down my own destructive barriers at a young age after recognizing my lack of confidence.

But never would I share with him that my high school counselor tried to destroy the foundation he worked years to establish. She did not hesitate to tell me that medical school was extremely competitive and that I might have thought about nursing instead. I felt defeated— since she was an African American female, I thought she must have known the odds. I would never discuss this with my father because I did not want to disappoint him by telling him that this dream we built may not happen; also, he might have gone to the school and had a few words with her if he thought she was wrong. I decided to leave my faith in my dad and pray he was right. Why should I have believed her? I only met with her a few times a year, and she had not really become invested in my goals through our superficial conversations about my dreams.

Children's instincts can be precise, especially when adults and parents are consistent with their trust. A "daddy's girl" I am. My daddy represents love, wisdom, patience, security, confidence, hard work, spirituality, loyalty, and unconditional love. Also, when needed, he showed me that strong men cry, too.

# Chapter 4

## My Maternal and Fear Journey

*"We are not fighting for integration, nor are we fighting for separation. We are fighting for recognition as human beings...In fact, we are actually fighting for rights that are even greater than civil rights and that is human rights."*

- Malcolm X

It was past dusk. The temperature was perfect. People crowded the street. It was a celebration. I saw myself beyond the chatter and music, sitting alone on the paved street, legs extended in my wedding dress. A whimsical young African American toddler walked toward me from a short distance away. *Did he know me? Why was he so trusting of me? Would he turn away and abandon me? Where was his mom?*

He enthusiastically straddled my legs and clasped my torso. Instantaneously, I was overwhelmed with the joy that radiated from my heart and spread to every cell in my body. I embraced him back, hoping to keep this positive neurologic surge of emotion that I only felt before in a dream of my biological mother. She came to me in a dream years after her death while I was at the lowest point in medical school after losing my father. In a moment of fear in my dream, she comforted me with a hug and reminded me that she would never let anything happen to me.

The hug was like a jump to a car battery, a hit of heroin to a dope fiend. My mother was taken from me by cancer when I was six, and I could not remember how her hugs felt until that dream and now again in this dream about my unborn son. I never knew before that moment what it felt like to experience a hug from my child because he would not be born for almost two years. It was wonderful! At that moment, I knew that he was mine—my "sun." A radiant being of life was revealed to me before his birth. He was a light in a dark world that would ignite forever.

When I woke up from that dream of our son, I told my husband about it. For the next couple of years, until his birth, he visited both of us in our dreams on special dates.

On the afternoon of Friday, August 9, 2002, I was overcome with a warm, reassuring maternal desire. Prior to this, my conversations with my husband had confirmed that I was not ready to start a family. I was in my third year of an extremely vigorous pediatric residency in Detroit. There was only time to work. It was not uncommon to work eighty hours in a week. Sleep and eating were considered luxuries. So, I walked up to him and said, "Ok, now is the time. I am ready for us to try to have a baby."

He did not believe me, so he laughed and said, "Are you joking?", with a grin but a touch of uncertainty. I knew this feeling was not going to last long, so I had to confirm that aliens had not taken over my body to start procreating and take over the world. Also, I was thirty-one years old and was not getting any younger. This would be the perfect time since I was ovulating—before approaching my husband, I had already calculated the expected due date to be one day before my birthday. There could not be a better time since I was graduating from residency in June. I would give birth, make up my maternity time, start working for a private practice on the east coast and not need to ask for maternity leave. That is every private practice's dream candidate.

In that instant, in the middle of our living room, after my husband confirmed that I was sober and lucid, we made love intentionally and without any barriers. As we concluded, I blurted, "Grab some pillows!" as our love began to flow out. He placed them beneath my lower back and sacral area to flex my hips while I held my legs in the air to welcome at least one of my husband's sperm.

We talked and laughed about my sudden change of mind and all thoughts that ran through his mind for approximately thirty minutes to allow the sperm to find its way into my cervix. We prayed, and it was done. I believe our lives were predestined by a higher power. My husband and I, like many other parents, were chosen by God for this assignment. Our son was revealed to us in our dreams before conception to prepare us mentally. Parenting is a gift that requires courage, strength, wisdom, love, discipline, dedication, understanding, faith, and selflessness. These are the qualities we all aspire to achieve.

**The commencement of life**

"Wake," my mind commands my paralyzed body on the morning

of August 23rd. Today is the day that my menstrual cycle should begin. I lie as motionless as possible as my mind searches to detect if the thunderous roar has begun in my pelvis. There is no routine cramping radiating to my back. There is an absence of the warm fullness of my girth that will take over my body, causing an assortment of emotions or cravings. The workday has ended, and the inquiries enter my mind, but my body has not shown any evidence of the cycle it has been accustomed to for over seventeen years.

Again, again, morning to night. After a week, I sat over the commode with the scientific wand. I drenched it to assure my purchase was a good investment—I was a pediatric resident and made less than minimum wage based on my hours worked. In this world of instant results, even this method could not reassure my pessimistic tendencies at that moment, thus causing my sympathetic nervous system to surge. Finally, the fluid reaches the end of the litmus paper. At first, there is one dark pink line, and then my eyes focus on a second faint pink line. I run to my husband and place the stick enthusiastically in his face. He moves it back gently to a comfortable distance and grins.

I enthusiastically schedule my prenatal visits and ensure that we are on time, following every word of my doctor's orders. I go for my ultrasound. The technician is an older lady, possibly in her fifties, and she recognizes that I am one of the pediatric residents from the hospital. She confirms everything looks good—our son's cord is wrapped once around his neck, but this will not pose a problem. She shares that she has been performing ultrasounds for years, and the residents' cervices always seem to thin prematurely, so I should beware. I reflect on her words through daily routines of running upstairs and down hallways in response to beepers demanding my immediate service to a distressed newborn delivery, code blue, or expected trauma flown in from across the state. I recall the concern of injury to my unborn child when exposed to flailing extremities of children fearful of procedures I was about to perform on them. The long, vigorous stress-filled hours on our feet contribute to premature delivery and sometimes demise. I instantly hear whispers of my colleagues having miscarriages.

I am in my twenty-eighth week of pregnancy, and a crescendo of excitement overwhelms me as I sign out to the next resident after a thirty-hour shift. My husband, a close friend, and I are headed to Maryland to my baby shower after the repeat ultrasound that I requested to check the cord around my son's neck. The hospital was busy the night before, and I was the house senior, so I did not sleep. I realized that I hardly drank anything my entire shift before I rushed to the ultrasound department and lay on the table. As the house senior, I supervised the first- and second-year residents, attended all codes and accepted the most acutely ill children transferred overnight by medevac from local hospitals from around the state. Along with the charge nurse and ER physician, your duty was to maintain all emergencies and stabilize all patients at night until the attending physicians returned in the morning to do rounds on the patients. I anxiously get dressed after my ultrasound, which was performed by the same technician from months ago. I check my watch. I have been in the room for over twenty minutes. A resident comes in and explains that my cervix has thinned. My doctor requests an exam, lab work, and monitoring. I am devastated that my son is in danger of premature delivery at twenty-eight weeks, which would not give his lungs and other organs enough time to develop.

My obstetrician and sorority sister sentenced me to ten weeks of bed rest. It does not take long to get over the sacrifice and disappointment of canceling the shower to allow my son's lungs to develop appropriately before use and reduce the chance that he will need a ventilator to survive. The silver lining is that a record-breaking snow blizzard hit the east coast that weekend. Had I traveled to Maryland not knowing I was in premature labor, I might not have made it to the hospital for a safe delivery. But I often reflect on how appreciative I am to my Black female obstetrician's personal care in assuring that immediate actions be taken, such as taking me out of work and monitoring his movements with daily readings which saved my son's life and possibly my own. We made it to the end. A healthy baby boy was delivered. Motherhood had begun.

I breastfed what felt like every hour as I studied for my boards while sleep-deprived and trying to remember when I last ate. I was exhausted and feeling numb. I remember reading an article about Jada Pinkett Smith's postpartum experience. Jada, the same age as me and also a native of Baltimore, was a trusted messenger in her writing of my struggles to keep up with the new demands of motherhood while dwelling hundreds of miles away from my supportive family.

My eyes were opened as I was allowed to view myself under

this anesthetic stupor, conscious now that I was alive but passing the hours as a helpless zombie. *How do I get control?* I would take my son for strolls around the neighborhood so I could get fresh air and view new scenery. I would sit him in his chair on the table alongside my books or on my breast for a meal and read my medical literature to him while I studied.

When my husband arrived home from work, I got my grocery list together, left the house, and returned refreshed. Acknowledging Jada's story was a blessing. I never forget to reassure new mothers when they come for their first visits that they are great mothers and give them the guidance needed to recognize that and get through. I completed my last few months of pediatric residency and returned to the east coast, where both my and my husband's families resided and could support us.

**No room for mistakes**

Suddenly, I became more aware of some deep trauma rooted within. I questioned myself, *Stacey, why are you so concerned about your son's path?* I realized I had witnessed some negative experiences that forced me to wonder how I could better prepare and protect my son. Education was at the forefront even though my journey through high school was bearable as a female.

One thing I realized through my educational journey is that school curricula, ethics, and philosophies such as all children should be challenged on an academic level are in place to encourage students to excel. The schools I attended all encouraged me to work harder. I was afforded the opportunity to learn and form bonds with the brightest

Black males during elementary and middle school.

**Trauma 1**

The physical protection of my son's life started rising to the top of the list of my priorities as he grew from a toddler to school age. I am now ready to share my trauma. It all started one September day in 1991 when I returned to my college dorm room and received a phone call that would forever change my life—a phone call that forced me to question if it was real, to wonder if a devastation like an earthquake had fractured my being forever. My best friend since the age of five had suffered a family tragedy. We had made a pact in elementary school that we would not allow any obstacles to block our path to becoming physicians. We attended elementary, middle, and high school together, practically living in one another's homes like sisters. We recently separated to attend college in two different states, twelve hours apart. We both planned to pledge to the same sorority and share any information needed to be successful.

The call I received was to inform me that her brother—and my brother by association—Sadiq, had been killed by a police officer. I could not fathom what my ears were asking my brain to process. Who could commit such a heinous act of violence against a teenager?

I rushed back to be by the side of my friend and family as funeral arrangements were made and justice was demanded. Ceaseless tears, heartache, and rage overwhelmed me as reality set in when I entered their home, and he was not present. I was not greeted by his smile, joking, and signature teasing (as perfected by all younger brothers to torture you with). Boyz II Men's song "It's So Hard to Say Goodbye to Yesterday" played in the background on the radio as a group of us reunited, seeking refuge in one another. This was the first time I had ever heard this song, and it still brings instant tears whenever I hear it. Sadiq was laid to rest, but justice did not prevail despite the FBI being called in for an investigation.

**Trauma 2**

A decade later, another tragedy occurred. My younger cousin, Kenneth, was born during my early teen years in Prince George's County of Maryland. I considered Kenneth my baby. I would stay at his home for weeks during summer break and on occasional weekends during the school year to spend time with him and his family.

Kenneth was the product of a love-filled biracial marriage. He was raised as an only child in a suburban neighborhood. He attended public school and graduated from high school, and he was loved by his peers. He made his parents proud, especially when he entered college in the fall.

My last memories with Kenneth are of the time we spent together during Christmas break of his first year of college, just a few weeks before his death. My husband and I had traveled from Michigan, where I was completing my pediatric residency. I had only a few days to spend but made it a point to stop by to spend a little time with Kenneth. It was wonderful because we were able to have a quality conversation. We spoke of his goals and, most importantly, of his plan to navigate through this phase of his life. My goal in our conversation was for him to recognize the incredible life experience his parents had worked hard to afford him.

As he spoke of his friends and empathized with their lives saying things like "it's a hard life out here", I quickly realized that his friends' situations were different from his. Explaining that his parents poured everything into him before thinking of themselves, I warned him how jealousy could bring out the worst in a person. "Kenneth, you have everything your friends would ever want," I told him. "You are a college student, own your own car, and have two loving parents who wake up and go to bed with their love for you on their mind. All of your wants and needs have been met without you lifting a finger. You are handsome, intelligent, and full of personality. You have it all." He smiled and assured me that these friends were good to him and were like brothers.

One month later, nothing could have prepared me for the phone call I received from his mother, Vickie. "Kenneth is dead," she said, crying. "Someone killed him, Stacey." Kenneth's friends came to his home to comfort his parents and told them they were dedicated to finding out who murdered Kenneth. After the authorities investigated the incident and questioned witnesses, it was found that his trusted "friend" was the assailant. He had murdered Kenneth in his car with a gunshot to his head in January 2002. Kenneth's life was taken by someone he considered amongst his "brotherhood" through his standards. His murderer lost sight of the meaning of the commitment of this level of friendship, either because he let jealousy or hate conquer his values or because he had never experienced true friendship, the kind where someone loves you without expectations. This type of friendship possesses the Greek phileo love, which requires a deep connection. Jealousy and envy are the poisons that ruin the potential for brotherhood.

His murderer still serves time in jail, left to reevaluate his actions. He had experienced the overflow of love from Kenneth's family while eating at his parent's table just weeks before Kenneth's death. He had ridden in Kenneth's car, which had been bought by Kenneth's parents. He had even shown up at their home after his death, deceivingly promising his parents he would find out who had done this to Kenneth. What type of human exhibits this type of conscienceless behavior? Yes, he is someone's son as well, but has he truly been properly rehabilitated to go back into society and live alongside other citizens? Could this be possible? I believe so, but that is not the goal of our justice system.

**Trauma 3**

A decade-and-a-half later, tragedy would strike again. It was early morning August 17, 2016. I received a voice message as my plane landed after a return flight from dropping my children in Alabama at an overnight space camp. It was my cousin, asking that I return her call as soon as possible. I knew this was not a routine call, but I never dreamed I would hear the words she would say next- "Bruce was shot at the BP gas station around the corner last night." I knew this gas station very well and the change in its reputation over the decades. I know the neighborhood of Sandtown in Baltimore city well, not only because my maternal aunt and uncle lived there for over sixty years but also because I spent my entire second-grade year there, one year after the death of my mother to cancer.

I lived with my aunt and cousins to ensure my safety since I was young and my father was transitioning into a job with varying hours. The previous year, I had been a "latchkey kid," along with many of my other friends. While our parents worked, we routinely entered our homes independently, made lunch, and finished our homework. Junior high school's dismissal time was about forty minutes later than the elementary school's to allow the younger children to make their way home first. So, my brother would arrive within the hour to supervise until my dad came home from work.

Moving to Sandtown meant I would have to make new friends and meet new teachers. My aunt worked as a school crossing guard at my elementary school by day and under my great-aunt as a nurse at a nearby nursing home in the evenings. My aunt was known by everyone who dwelled in Sandtown because she had helped generations of children in the neighborhood cross the major two-lane street as the cars traveled south to downtown Baltimore, allowing the children to arrive home safely. Over the decades, Sandtown, like other neighborhoods, became the victim of neglect from its political system.

The last of my aunt's grandchildren, male twins, were born while I was in medical school. The twins captured my heart as infants with their unique personalities. Bruce, known to family and close friends as BJ, was a bubbly, wide-eyed boy full of life who loved socializing. Bruce and I found a common point of interest in math. Once this became apparent, whenever I saw him, I would ask what new math topic he was studying, and we would spend time getting lost in equations and math trivia.

I watched both twins grow and mature into young men while realizing my young son revered his older cousins. What a joyous moment it was when we celebrated Bruce's high school graduation, just two months before his death and just a few weeks after the death of his cherished grandfather, my uncle. Bruce was so proud of his accomplishments because not many of his Black male peers were so lucky. I had the opportunity to speak with both twins at Bruce's graduation celebration, which was hosted by the family. He was so enthusiastic about his future. When I asked what he planned to do with his life, his eyes lit up, and he said, "I just want a job!" He was not sure what type of job, but the idea that he was coming of age, had earned his diploma, and could work was a badge of honor to him.

Every year, our family met up on the Eastern Shore of Maryland for our treasured annual family reunion. This gathering is the glue that holds us together. My grandmother initiated this affair, and other matriarchs took the torch in her name after her passing. Love, music, celebrations of milestones and birthdays, food, memories, and—last but not least—crabs fueled the anticipation for this weekend-long event year after year. One week after our annual family reunion, and one year almost to the day of the death of Freddie Gray and just about a mile away in the same neighborhood, Bruce's life was taken by a familiar assailant. So many of our Black male's lives are taken each year in this very zip code. Young innocent children have been injured in the crossfire while playing as children should.

However, the streets will never whisper the murderer's name or turn him in to authorities after the stop snitchin' movement spread through a video made in Baltimore in the early 2000s. This code had been on the streets before the video and acts of terror had been perpetrated against citizens, such as Angela Dawson of Baltimore. Angela was killed after her house was firebombed in response to her reporting drug deals in her neighborhood. She was killed along with her husband and five children.

On the night of Bruce's assassination, witnesses surrounded his body before his twin could arrive to hold his brother in his arms. EMS arrived on the scene to revive and transport Bruce's lifeless body to the hospital. A witness explained that a child from the neighborhood had stood nearby watching the ambulance as it approached the next block; the driver then turned the lights and sirens off. He looked as if he was unaffected by the gruesome scene and violent act that had just occurred. He simply uttered, "They turned the lights off. He didn't make it." This elementary school-age Black boy had experienced the scene of a homicide so many times that he processed the protocol followed by the professionals with an apathetic disposition.

After my plane arrived back in Baltimore, I dropped my personal belongings off at home and headed to my aunt's home, where our family and close friends had gathered to comfort each other. My children were away, and I struggled to decide what words I would use to explain to my middle-school-aged son, upon his return, that the life of one of his adored cousins had been snuffed out.

Sadiq, Kenneth, and Bruce were now gone, along with many other Black males across many cities, including some that I had attended school with. My life has not been the same since their deaths. I remained very disciplined in writing this book in hopes of changing the fate of today's young men.

Maternal Instinct is a book intended to start conversations that will change the narrative of Black males in America by providing them with a strategy that they can follow to increase their chances of continuing to compete and earn a seat at the table while acknowledging persistent inequities. I lost three young Black loved ones within months of graduating high school. Two of them lost their lives to other Black males who looked like them. These murderers used the only thing they had over their victims: the will to give themselves POWER. That meant taking the life of another person because jealousy and disappointment had overtaken them when their family, the broken education system, and society had become too much to face. As a result, they can't stand to look into the eyes of another Black male who has everything he ever wanted.

# PART II

## STRATEGIES

*"Healing begins where the wound was made."*

*-Alice Walker*

# Chapter 5

## Education

*"Oppressive language does more than represent violence; it is violence; does more than represent the limits of knowledge; it limits knowledge."*

**-Toni Morrison**

The initiation of learning with a child as early as possible is important because it sets the foundation for their future intellectual, emotional, and social development. Here are some reasons why:

- Brain Development: During the early years of a child's life, their brain is rapidly developing and forming neural connections that will shape their cognitive abilities throughout their lifetime. Research has shown that the earlier a child is exposed to learning experiences, the stronger their brain development will be.

- Learning Readiness: Early learning experiences help children develop the skills and abilities they need to be ready to learn more complex concepts in the future. For example, early literacy experiences can help children develop language

- and reading skills that will be essential for academic success later on.

- Socialization: Early learning experiences can also help children develop social skills and emotional intelligence. When children are exposed to learning experiences early, they have more opportunities to interact with other children and adults, learn how to cooperate, and develop social skills.

- Lifelong Learning: By fostering a love of learning at an early age, children are more likely to become lifelong learners. They will be more curious, more willing to explore new ideas and concepts, and more motivated to continue learning throughout their lives.

In short, initiating learning with a child as early as possible provides a strong foundation for their overall development and sets them up for success in the future.

As part of early initiation, mothers can read to their fetuses for bonding purposes and possible prenatal enrichment. Since my obstetrician placed me on bed rest for ten weeks at twenty-eight weeks gestational age while carrying my son, I purchased a book entitled *Good Night Moon* to read to my son, in addition to the medical books I read for myself. I would read this book with exclamation once or twice a day. After ten weeks of reading to him while on bed rest and upon arriving home and settling in, I read the book to my son. He turned his head reflexively to my reading. I was in disbelief, so I later asked my husband to witness my reading and my son's reaction. I was convinced, continued to read to him regularly, and continued the tradition with my next pregnancy with my daughter, with similar results. Reading to your son daily is a wonderful habit that allows you to bond and enrich your son's language comprehension.

It is never too early to initiate learning with your son. Toddlers are taught sign language to express themselves when there is a delay in their speech to enhance their social skills. There are no limits to what you can expose your children to. Word recognition, alphabet sounds, and phonics are not out of reach. Myelination of a toddler's brain occurs during this stage at a rapid pace. It is recommended to assist this process by giving your child fat in their diet, which is found in whole milk (as opposed to reduced-fat milk). If dairy is not an option, there are many other ways to get fat into your child's diet. It is recommended to decrease the amount of fat after two years of age if desired.

My son is my firstborn, and I admit to using him as my prototype. I started teaching him his alphabet and letters as a toddler. There is a specific DVD we exposed him to, and I often recommend it to my patients' parents who are interested in early education. By two years of age, my son could recite and recognize each letter, and when asked, he could give its sound. By thirty months of age, he could put letter sounds together to read short rhyming words.

If toddlers can sing songs from the radio in their entirety, that same brain can learn to read, recognize colors and count in most cases. Parents must hold themselves accountable during these initial stages to give their children this advantage. Many cultures have been doing this for years. Economics does not have to play a substantial role in this process. All you need is paper, a pencil, and time.

I do not agree with sitting children in front of the television, phone, or computer for learning for extended time intervals since human interaction is extremely necessary for proper language development. A critical stage of language development for toddlers is the transition from repetitive speech, also known as echolalia. This is when you state something to a toddler and he or she repeats it back to you. A higher level of communication is when they are able to place words together with purpose. If large amounts of time are spent listening and repeating phrases from a computer versus through interactive communication, expressive language may be compromised. Infants even babble, then pause to wait for your response and babble again when there is silence. Even at this stage, they are learning cues of communication through their parent's facial expressions, tone, and language.

Limit your son's electronics, computer, and television time to fewer hours a day. Fill in the extra time with personal communication, exercise, and reading. Ensure that your son gets at least ten hours of sleep. Always reward your son for his efforts and attention, even when he may not have the correct response, with phrases such as "good try," "you are close," or "great job." Be sure to know your son's limits and know when to back off.

Limiting your child's electronic, computer, and television time can be challenging in today's digital age, but it's important for their overall health and well-being. Here are some strategies that may help:

- Set Limits: Establish clear rules and expectations around screen time, including how much time your child is allowed to spend on electronic devices each day. You may want to consider using a timer to help your child stay on track.

- Encourage Alternative Activities: Encourage your child to engage in other activities that don't involve screens, such as reading, playing outside, or participating in sports or other hobbies.

- Model Healthy Behaviors: Children learn by example, so make sure you're modeling healthy screen habits yourself. Set aside time to unplug and engage in other activities, and be mindful of how much time you're spending on screens around your child.

- Create Screen-Free Zones: Consider creating screen-free zones in your home, such as the dining room or bedrooms, to help limit your child's exposure to screens.

- Use Parental Controls: Use parental controls on your child's devices to limit their access to inappropriate content and to set time limits on their usage.

- Be Consistent: Consistency is key when it comes to setting limits on screen time. Stick to your rules and expectations and be prepared to enforce consequences if your child breaks them.

- Encourage Family Time: Instead of using screens for entertainment, encourage your family to spend time together engaging in activities like playing board games, cooking, or doing arts and crafts.

- Use Screen Time as a Reward: Use screen time as a reward for good behavior, completing chores, or reaching academic goals. This can help your child understand that screen time is a privilege, not a right.

- Be Mindful of Screen Use During Meals: Avoid using screens during meals, as it can disrupt family conversations and discourage healthy eating habits.

- Find Educational Apps and Programs: Look for educational apps and programs that can help your child learn while still engaging with screens. This can be a great way to promote learning and limit screen time at the same time.

- Get Outside: Encourage your child to spend time outside, playing with friends or exploring nature. Outdoor activities are a great way to promote physical activity and reduce screen time.

Remember that screen time is not all bad, and there are many educational and beneficial uses for electronic devices and television. However, it's important to find a healthy balance and prioritize other activities that promote physical activity, socialization, and creative thinking. Limiting screen time doesn't have to be a punishment.

I am a strong believer that the preschool experience gives children an advantage over their peers. They are acclimated to the routine and structure of a classroom. They are also equipped with social skills such as peer interactions, sharing, task completion, and expectations of attention and following rules. Preschool teachers often design their curricula around teaching self-help, imaginative play, enhancing motor skills and problem-solving, and exposure to arithmetic and literacy. Certain learning or speech delays are discovered in preschool that may have been missed and might require individualized educational plans. If followed by a pediatrician on a regular schedule as an infant and toddler, most developmental delays are revealed through special screening tools called the Ages and Stages Questionnaire (ASQ) and the Modified Checklist for Autism in Toddlers (M-CHAT).

Preschool advantages cross socioeconomic differences and attrition, which, if not offered, may put some subgroups at a disadvantage. The Chicago Longitudinal Study documented the development of fifteen hundred families, the majority of whom were

African American and nine hundred of whom participated in the Child-Parent-Center Education Program, the second oldest preschool program in Chicago's public school system. The study showed that access to early education can increase opportunities for higher education, increase a child's levels of social economics, and decrease the chances that a child will get involved in the judicial system and substance abuse. The students in the preschool group achieved higher levels of education as indicated by outcomes such as highest grade completed. Follow-ups with these students until they were twenty-eight years old showed that the preschool group achieved higher economic status based on their occupational prestige, higher socioeconomic status, and income.

The findings also showed the most influence in males and economically disadvantaged children. Children of mothers without high school diplomas enrolled in the preschool group were successful and, when compared to non-preschool children of mothers without diplomas, committed fewer felonies and were victims of substance abuse far less often.

The argument for funding preschools for males of color is clear. Males of color have become an endangered species. There is major attrition and disparity amongst males of color in the United States. President Barack Obama's My Brother's Keeper Initiative was an attempt to give males of color a chance to fight before being faced with the many pitfalls in their path. As taxpayers, we have a choice to either invest in preschool for children, which will advance our nation, or continue to build prisons for disadvantaged children who are often left to fight alone (the only way they know how) when they are pushed onto the next grade level. When we witness fewer males incarcerated, families will thrive with men who can once again earn an honest living because they are confident due to the equal educational opportunities and high institutional expectations given by school boards.

There are a few subclasses in the school system that are often not announced formally. There was a change in the etiquette of the educational system some twenty years ago to integrate children with learning disabilities. In recent years, some school districts have quietly integrated gifted and talented students into classrooms with hopes that their peers do not notice a difference. The students seem to know, but I wonder if it may merely be a camouflage for parents. "Gifted and talented" is a classification some educational systems use to recognize students with advanced intellect in specific areas. Characteristics of a gifted learner are an excellent memory, unusual alertness, the ability to learn quickly, the ability to associate atypical concepts, vivid imaginations, abstract curiosity, ability to self-teach after an introduction of a subject, and the enjoyment of mental stimulation in the area in which the individual is gifted.

Understand that gifted students may be gifted in only one area. It may take extra effort from gifted students' parents to expose their children to other subjects. In these less-attractive school subjects, the child's brain can be conditioned like a muscle, and weaknesses can be overcome. It is important to exercise the various areas of learning to strengthen his intellectual abilities. This will make him a more well-rounded student.

It is also important to understand that gifted children may possess traits that mimic hyperactivity and emotional sensitivity. Kazimierz Dabrowski, a psychiatrist and psychologist, founded the theory of positive disintegration. He theorized that if an individual possesses characteristics of special talents or abilities such as high-level intellect, athletic or musical/artistic ability, along with a strong internal drive and overexcitability, they are considered to have an advanced development.

Some gifted individuals may possess advanced development and overexcitability. These sensitive sensory stimuli are categorized as psychomotor, sensual, intellectual, imaginational, and emotional. Psychomotor OEs are hyperactivity, impulsivity, and talkativeness. These are often misdiagnosed as attention deficit hyperactivity disorder (ADHD). Sensory OEs are hypersensitivity to sensory stimuli, either positively or negatively. Gifted children generally possess some form of intellectual OE and exhibit an unusual ability to sustain focus on problem-solving or pondering issues involving moral inequalities. Imaginational OE individuals are dreamers and have vivid visual abilities. Children with emotional OE possess an intense expression of feeling. So, keep this in mind if your son shows hyperactive qualities but is able to excel in his core subjects.

Overall, African American males graduate at lower rates in the United States than White and Latino males per the Schott 50

State Report on Public Education and Black Males. Idaho, Maine, New Jersey, Arizona, and South Dakota were found to have the highest rates of Black male graduation, all higher than 75%. Georgia, Michigan, Nevada, Ohio, Louisiana, Indiana, Mississippi, South Carolina, Nebraska, and the District of Columbia ranked the lowest, all less than 55%. The highest Black male graduation rates in the nation, by region, were 75% in Newark (NJ), 69% in Montgomery County (MD), 67% in Baltimore County (MD), 64% in Fort Bend (TX), 61% in Cumberland County (NC), 57% in Guilford County (NC), and 55% in Prince George's County (MD). The lowest rates were 29% in Duval (FL) and Richmond County (GA); 28% in Cleveland (OH), New York City (NY), Pinellas County (FL), and Chatham (GA); 27% in Clark County (NV); 26% in Philadelphia (PA); 23% in Detroit (MI); and 21% in Rochester (NY). In Detroit, 13% of White males graduated, which is less than the 23% Black males who graduated.

On the 2013 NAEP Grade 8 Math Assessment, 13% of Black males, 21% of Latino males, and 45% of White males scored at or above proficiency. Also, 13% of Black males, 17% of Latino males, and 38% of White males scored at or above proficiency on the reading test.

I am unsure if anyone is keeping up, but in some states, this should be considered child neglect, and these school districts should be held somewhat accountable. Children spend forty hours a week in a classroom, with learning as one of its major purposes. What is missing? The system should stop, reevaluate, and revise a plan to ensure that no child is excluded.

**Keeping it real**

Over my eighteen-plus years in pediatric medicine, I have treated patients who now entrust me with the health of their children. My practice spans families from diverse ethnic and socioeconomic backgrounds. I help children diagnosed with congenital defects, developmental delays, in utero narcotic drug exposure, ADHD, depression, obesity, and various medical illnesses. My patient families are made of two-parent and one-parent households, as well as children living with their grandparents or extended family members, foster parents, and surrogate parents from single-sex or heterosexual relationships from professional, working-class families with support, as well as others with food insecurity, homelessness, and poverty. None of these factors determine the outcome of children's success. I would not be writing this book if some of these factors did not build obstacles for children to achieve success.

In my practice, all children benefit from my sensitive awareness of disparities, which are present in middle- and upper-class families, as well as among the less fortunate. Several working families have less time to role model because they have less quality time to spend with their children after school, leaving children with resources that may allow for distractions and sometimes downfalls. With time, I have witnessed many changes in the education system's curriculum, educational plans for children with learning disabilities, bullying, and adaptability to various learning styles alongside a decline in effective discipline for corrective behaviors. Schools are becoming overcrowded, buildings are in need of revitalization, and the increased behavior diagnoses in children are making it challenging to create a positive learning environment.

Many schools are allotted budgets for children with individual education plans (IEPs) and 504 plans. This can make it challenging for administrators in certain high-risk districts to accommodate potential students in need. Criteria for qualifications, available resources, and budgets may vary based on state, county, and city. The choice between private schools and public schools may also be difficult for parents, and they must investigate their options before enrolling their children. I encourage all families to get to know the intentions of their school boards, get involved, express their opinions in writing to their superintendents, and vote for the candidate that they agree with. The first step is getting involved in your child's school by becoming a member of the parent-teacher association (PTA) and scheduling regular conferences with teachers at least once per quarter. Get feedback on your child's performance and behavior. Address any concerns with your child and teacher present to assure everyone is on the same page, and always leave with a plan for improvement.

Education is only one area of importance to ensure your child has a good start in life. Maintaining their health through yearly well-child visits with your pediatrician is essential. Health maintenance is important for your child to attend school regularly by avoiding unnecessary hospitalizations and injuries. Also, many developmental delays and learning disabilities are often caught by your child's pediatrician while your child is still an infant or toddler, thus providing the best opportunity for enrichment through speech therapy, occupational therapy, and physical therapy. Be sure that your child's pediatrician communicates effectively with you regarding the disease in terms that you understand. It may take a few visits for you to get a full understanding, but following up is extremely important if you want to see progress. You are the custodian of your child's health and are ultimately responsible for ensuring they remain in good health.

Take a look at checklist on the following pages to help ensure a good education for young boys:

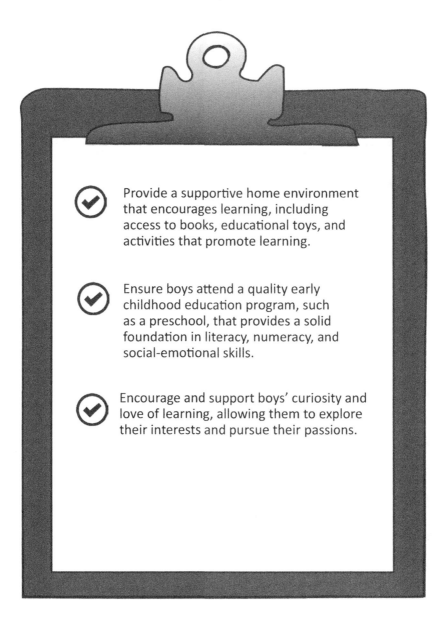

Provide a supportive home environment that encourages learning, including access to books, educational toys, and activities that promote learning.

Ensure boys attend a quality early childhood education program, such as a preschool, that provides a solid foundation in literacy, numeracy, and social-emotional skills.

Encourage and support boys' curiosity and love of learning, allowing them to explore their interests and pursue their passions.

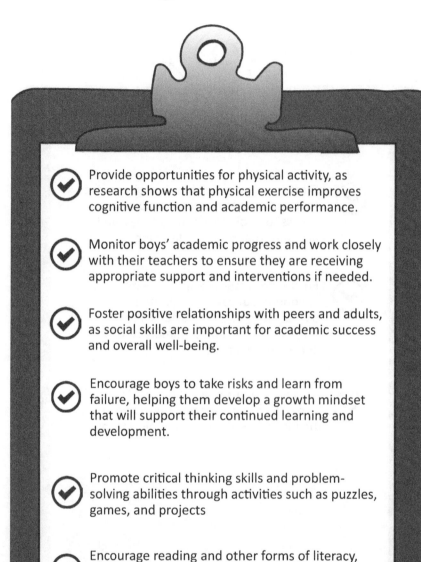

Provide opportunities for physical activity, as research shows that physical exercise improves cognitive function and academic performance.

Monitor boys' academic progress and work closely with their teachers to ensure they are receiving appropriate support and interventions if needed.

Foster positive relationships with peers and adults, as social skills are important for academic success and overall well-being.

Encourage boys to take risks and learn from failure, helping them develop a growth mindset that will support their continued learning and development.

Promote critical thinking skills and problem-solving abilities through activities such as puzzles, games, and projects

Encourage reading and other forms of literacy, including writing and speaking, as these skills are fundamental to success in all areas of life.

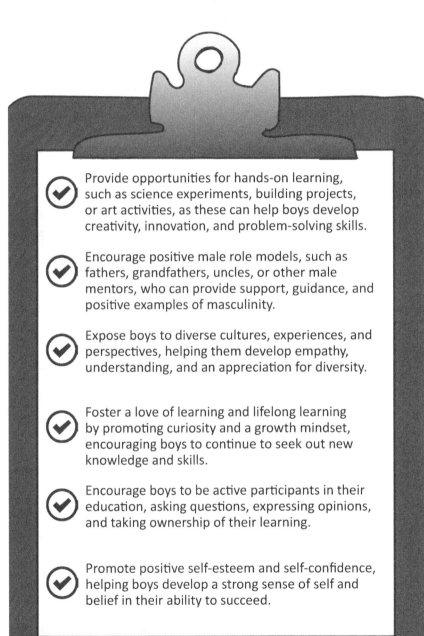

Provide opportunities for hands-on learning, such as science experiments, building projects, or art activities, as these can help boys develop creativity, innovation, and problem-solving skills.

Encourage positive male role models, such as fathers, grandfathers, uncles, or other male mentors, who can provide support, guidance, and positive examples of masculinity.

Expose boys to diverse cultures, experiences, and perspectives, helping them develop empathy, understanding, and an appreciation for diversity.

Foster a love of learning and lifelong learning by promoting curiosity and a growth mindset, encouraging boys to continue to seek out new knowledge and skills.

Encourage boys to be active participants in their education, asking questions, expressing opinions, and taking ownership of their learning.

Promote positive self-esteem and self-confidence, helping boys develop a strong sense of self and belief in their ability to succeed.

- ✅ Encourage boys to pursue their passions and interests, even if they are not traditionally associated with masculinity, such as music, art, or dance.

- ✅ Foster a sense of community and social responsibility, helping boys understand the importance of giving back and contributing to the world around them.

- ✅ Promote positive mental health and emotional well-being by teaching boys coping strategies for stress and anxiety, and encouraging open communication about feelings and emotions.

- ✅ Encourage boys to develop leadership skills, such as communication, collaboration, and decision-making, which can help them succeed in all areas of life.

- ✅ Provide opportunities for community service and volunteering, helping boys develop empathy, social awareness, and a sense of responsibility for the well-being of others.

# CHAPTER 5 | EDUCATION

Remember that education is not just about academic success, but also about developing well-rounded, empathetic, and responsible individuals who can contribute positively to society. By focusing on these broader goals, you can help ensure a good education for young boys that will serve them well throughout their lives. Keep in mind that every child is unique, and what works for one may not work for another. Be sure to adapt these guidelines to fit your child's individual needs and learning style.

# Chapter 6

## Brotherhood

*"In recognizing the humanity of our fellow beings, we pay ourselves the highest tribute."* -Thurgood Marshall

Brotherhood is a relationship between two or more people who support one another and share common interests. Not everyone has a brotherhood. In order to form a brotherhood, you must have the ability or desire to form a social bond with another human being. There are many benefits and undesirable outcomes of brotherhood. Benefits include friendship, support, confidence, healthy competition, companionship, protection, survival, motivation and positive mental health. Brotherhood can be incredibly important for Black boys as it provides a sense of belonging, support, and camaraderie. Black boys face unique challenges and experiences in society, such as systemic racism and discrimination, that can make it difficult for them to feel understood and valued. Brotherhood can provide a space where Black boys can connect with others who share similar experiences and can relate to their struggles.

Through brotherhood, Black boys can also learn important

life skills, such as effective communication, conflict resolution, and teamwork. They can support each other in achieving their goals and can serve as positive role models for each other. Additionally, brotherhood can help combat negative stereotypes and narratives that are often associated with Black boys. By building strong relationships with each other, Black boys can challenge these stereotypes understanding that through self-confidence, they are capable and resilient. Overall, brotherhood can provide Black boys with a sense of community and empowerment, helping them navigate the challenges of growing up and building a positive sense of self.

Some examples of brotherhood are sports teammates, fraternity brothers, religious or occupational organizations, group or video game chat groups and less attractive options of gangs. In this century, thanks to the internet, there are many extended forms of potential brotherhoods that do not require meeting in person. During the COVID-19 pandemic, our sons had more than their share of interactions over the internet. If your son is looking for brotherhood, one of the aforementioned groups may cross his path and meet his needs. In joining a brotherhood, his morals and beliefs should be reflected in the organization's creed.

You can teach your son to investigate before leaping. Run scenarios by him to see if he picks up clues that the group is a positive or negative influence. This is especially necessary if your son lives a sheltered life. Discernment and "street smarts" may be a strength needed while navigating life's journey. Each generation's experience is different from that of the one before. Today's young generation has unique complications related to the internet and social media. Their brains encounter thousands more stimuli in a day than our brains were subject to. Our children need to be able to process truth from fiction, filter important from irrelevant, practice self-control, and use good judgment as cyber laws unfold. Let's face it, they are exposed to brotherhoods in unfamiliar places, do not realize that their culture and experience are not the same, and support causes they don't have enough background to take a stand for. However, the internet is not always needed—this can take place in our own neighborhoods.

**Managing your expectations**

Children learn different skills in different environments. Often, we choose environments for our child's growth based on comfort, fear, economic reasons, diversity, or preconceived perceptions. Once in the environment, each child will explore until he or she finds a match. It is the parent's job to teach morality based on generational teachings, religion, and experience. Parents need to get to know the members who make up their sons' brotherhoods and, even more importantly, their parents or guardians. This provides you with a window through which you can view the new habits of your son and how they intertwine with your household teachings. If you are not careful, this could be counterproductive since he will spend most of his day with his peers at school or in other social and learning environments. Having conversations with your children about their beliefs regarding privileges, access to adult content, and academic and behavior expectations might give you a better reality and will require several interactions in most cases. Be respectful of possible age gaps or cultural differences of other families. Your son is watching, and you can learn volumes from him. Avoid prejudgment and give adequate time to see if this is destined to be a good fit. Openly discuss with other parents your values and teachings. Be authentic about any contrasts in child-rearing, giving the family an opportunity to make informed decisions about who they are comfortable with in connections.

Create realistic expectations for your son. Really get to know him, his likes and dislikes, personality, style, and strengths. The more you know about your child, the more you can guide him in the proper direction for his success. This is a healthy recipe for a healthy self-esteem. A healthy balance of your expectations is critical.

Overall, fostering brotherhood for Black sons requires a multifaceted approach that addresses various aspects of their lives. By encouraging self-expression, teaching financial literacy, promoting physical wellness, teaching critical thinking, celebrating cultural heritage, and building a network of support, parents can help their Black sons develop a strong sense of self and build meaningful relationships with other Black boys.

There are a few ways Black parents can foster brotherhood for their Black sons:

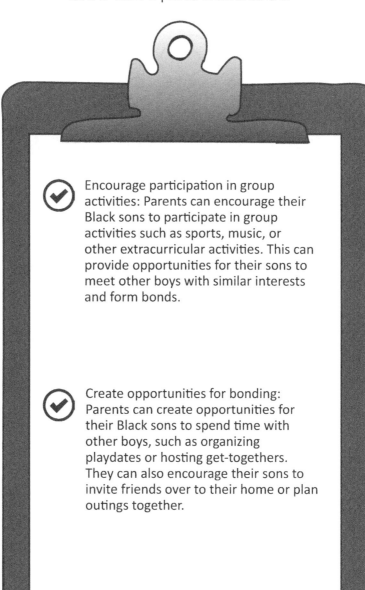

Encourage participation in group activities: Parents can encourage their Black sons to participate in group activities such as sports, music, or other extracurricular activities. This can provide opportunities for their sons to meet other boys with similar interests and form bonds.

Create opportunities for bonding: Parents can create opportunities for their Black sons to spend time with other boys, such as organizing playdates or hosting get-togethers. They can also encourage their sons to invite friends over to their home or plan outings together.

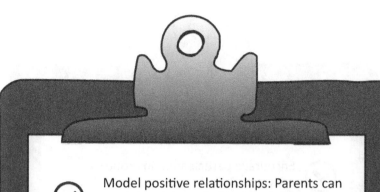

Model positive relationships: Parents can model positive relationships with other Black men and demonstrate the value of brotherhood. They can also teach their sons to be supportive, respectful, and caring towards their peers.

Teach conflict resolution skills: Parents can teach their Black sons effective communication and conflict resolution skills, which can help them build and maintain positive relationships with other boys.

Support community involvement: Parents can encourage their Black sons to get involved in their community and participate in programs or organizations

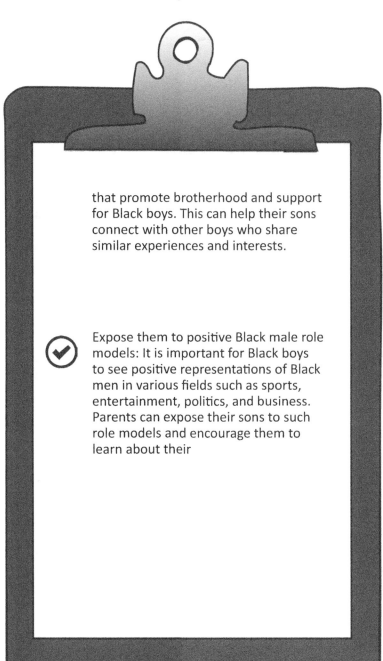

that promote brotherhood and support for Black boys. This can help their sons connect with other boys who share similar experiences and interests.

Expose them to positive Black male role models: It is important for Black boys to see positive representations of Black men in various fields such as sports, entertainment, politics, and business. Parents can expose their sons to such role models and encourage them to learn about their achievements, struggles, and values. This can help their sons develop a positive self-image and aspirations for the future.

 Emphasize the importance of education: Education can be a powerful tool for Black boys to overcome systemic barriers and achieve success. Parents can emphasize the importance of education and encourage their sons to pursue their academic goals. They can also provide resources and support to help their sons excel in school and prepare for college or career opportunities.

✓ Address toxic masculinity: Toxic masculinity can undermine brotherhood and lead to harmful behaviors such as aggression, violence, and disrespect towards women. Parents can educate their sons about healthy masculinity and promote values such as empathy, compassion, and respect for others. They can also address harmful behaviors and attitudes when they arise and provide guidance on how to treat others with kindness and fairness.

✓ Provide emotional support: Black boys may face unique emotional challenges such as navigating racial identity, coping with trauma, and dealing with social isolation. Parents can provide emotional support to their sons by listening to their concerns, validating their experiences, and offering guidance and resources. They can also encourage their sons to seek help from mental health professionals when needed.

Encourage self-expression: Black boys may face pressure to conform to narrow and harmful stereotypes about Black masculinity. Parents can encourage their sons to express themselves in ways that feel authentic and meaningful, whether it's through art, music, fashion, or

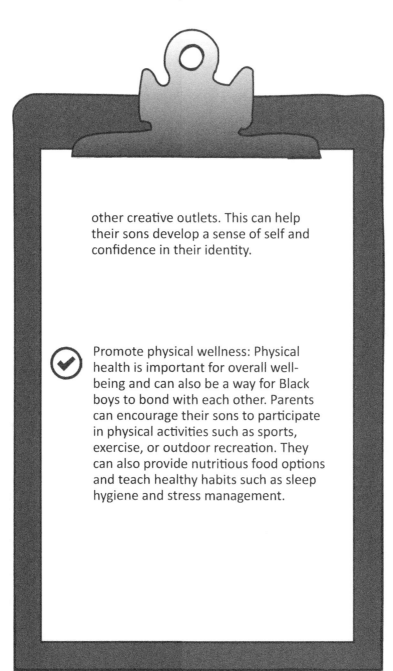

other creative outlets. This can help their sons develop a sense of self and confidence in their identity.

Promote physical wellness: Physical health is important for overall well-being and can also be a way for Black boys to bond with each other. Parents can encourage their sons to participate in physical activities such as sports, exercise, or outdoor recreation. They can also provide nutritious food options and teach healthy habits such as sleep hygiene and stress management.

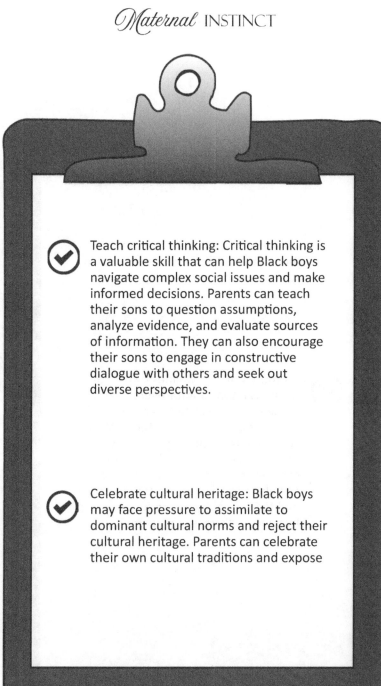

Teach critical thinking: Critical thinking is a valuable skill that can help Black boys navigate complex social issues and make informed decisions. Parents can teach their sons to question assumptions, analyze evidence, and evaluate sources of information. They can also encourage their sons to engage in constructive dialogue with others and seek out diverse perspectives.

Celebrate cultural heritage: Black boys may face pressure to assimilate to dominant cultural norms and reject their cultural heritage. Parents can celebrate their own cultural traditions and expose

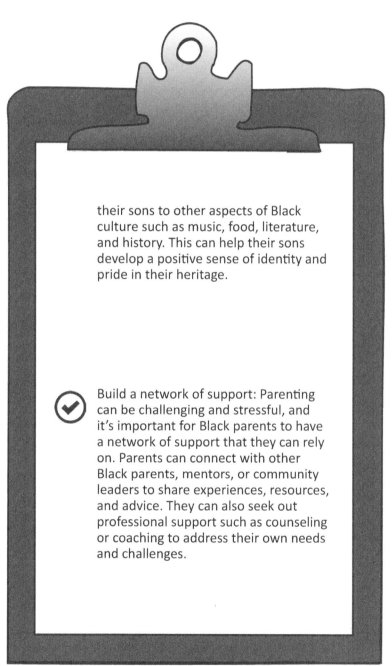

their sons to other aspects of Black culture such as music, food, literature, and history. This can help their sons develop a positive sense of identity and pride in their heritage.

Build a network of support: Parenting can be challenging and stressful, and it's important for Black parents to have a network of support that they can rely on. Parents can connect with other Black parents, mentors, or community leaders to share experiences, resources, and advice. They can also seek out professional support such as counseling or coaching to address their own needs and challenges.

# Chapter 7

## Economic Empowerment

*"Whatever we believe about ourselves and our ability comes true for us."*

-Susan L. Taylor

How do we rear our sons to value the concept of building wealth to assure stability for their family and future generations? Developing this mindset will position him to lay the foundation for his future family to elevate and flourish. He will establish wealth that will pass through generations of his seed, setting a family legacy.

You can teach your son how to govern his money appropriately by conserving, controlling, protecting, preserving, and supervising his wealth. Mothers can start by teaching their sons about the difference between needs and wants. Needs are the things that will sustain our existence. Wants are things we desire that are not deemed necessary. Our sons have learned as young as infancy how to express through crying his desire for the things he needs, such as food and a diaper change; however, through this, he has learned the pleasure of instant gratification, thus using this same method for his wants like being held or talked to on demand. By the time he is a toddler, he acts this out with tantrums and using words like "no" for his dislikes.

These learned behaviors leave us with the reality that we must remember to teach them as they grow the importance of money, how it is earned, and ways to profit from it. We can start the process early by saving a portion of the monetary gifts given to him at birthdays or special holidays. Invest these savings in creative ways to earn dollars for future wealth-building. As they grow, assigning chores is instrumental to teaching them the importance of a clean-living environment, community responsibility, and a sense of being an important part of a team, with or without an allowance. As young as two or three years old, they are able to clean up their toys and place them in an assigned toy chest with a reward of positive feedback such as a simple "good job." Toddlers love to hear these two words accompanied by a smile, positive tone, or a clapping gesture.

As they grow, kids often get a sense of entitlement and see their parents' benefits as their own without the understanding of how they were earned. This reasoning becomes unhealthy and solidifies the importance of chores and the transparency of earnings, bills, and budgets. In early grade school, children already begin learning the concepts of addition and subtraction, followed by the value of money. Often, to keep them occupied on long rides, my husband and I would engage our children in trivia games using money. We started with the unique differences between each coin, such as in their size, color, texture, and value. We then built up to real-world problems using imaginary scenarios such as familiar favorite items they like to purchase like stuffed animals or gum to determine the cost and change due to them after the exchange.

Understanding the value of money is only the first step in the algorithm. At younger ages, my children (like most) would ask for items at the store every chance they got, obviously not grasping that money is earned and that its purpose is to fund needs. One day in the store, I explained to my son that I did not have money to purchase something he wanted. He said, "Yes, you do. Just give him the card in your purse." At this moment, I became aware that he thought the amount of money on the card was infinite. This opened the conversation that income has a set dollar amount and that we have to budget the money we have after we pay for our needs like shelter, food, utilities, insurance, as well as our savings or investments. Only then can we buy some wants. This was a perfect situation to discuss the importance of setting career goals that align with his lifestyle expectations.

**Teaching financial health**

A lesson in delayed gratification is non-negotiable. This is a concept that many struggle with, including myself. We feel we earned money and that we should get possessions that we may want to express ourselves with. Our sons are watching this example from home, peers, or celebrities and focus their aspirations of acquiring things that place us in debt instead of things that appreciate in value. Thus, they fall into the trap of using credit without a purpose or plan. You see, credit does have its rewards if you plan to use it to eventually earn more wealth or to fund a need and pay it back responsibly. Our sons will be bombarded with credit card companies as soon as they turn eighteen without the means to pay off their debt. My father warned me not to apply for a credit card if I did not have the will to learn how to use it. I thought I understood but quickly realized I had no income while in college to pay this bill I had accumulated. I learned that lesson quickly, and I was blessed that he paid it off for me. We must warn our children of the traps of financial enslavement and student loan debt traps due to increasing tuition rates. We should encourage a proactive search for grants and scholarships to finance college and graduate school.

Teaching Black boys about the importance of financial health can be done in several ways, including:

Start early: It is important to start teaching children about financial health from a young age. Parents and guardians can involve children in everyday financial activities, such as grocery shopping, budgeting, and saving.

Use real-life examples: It is essential to use real-life examples to explain financial concepts. For example, show Black boys how to budget for a new video game or a sports equipment purchase.

Encourage saving: Encourage Black boys to save money regularly, even if it is just a small amount. This can be done by opening a savings account for them and setting a goal to save for a specific item.

Explain the importance of credit: It is important to explain the concept of credit and how it can impact their financial health in the future. Explain how credit scores work and how they can affect their ability to obtain a loan or credit card.

Teach about investing: Teach Black boys about investing in stocks, bonds, and other financial products. Explain the benefits of investing for long-term financial growth.

Provide positive role models: Provide Black boys with positive role models who exemplify good financial habits. This could be a family member, friend, or successful Black entrepreneur who has made smart financial decisions.

Overall, teaching Black boys about financial health is essential to their future success. By starting early, using real-life examples, encouraging saving, explaining credit, teaching about investing, and providing positive role models, you can help Black boys become financially savvy and responsible adults.

**Help your child to dream big**

My father was my sole advocate and ensured that I understood how important it was to dream at an early age. I shared my dreams of becoming a pediatrician with him, and he opened my mind further when he asked if I had thought of opening my own medical facility. He understood the power of entrepreneurship versus working for someone else, as he had experienced both. There is nothing wrong with being an employee, but he was teaching a little girl that nothing can limit you but yourself. This plan must have run through my head a million times.

Having someone I trusted believe in a dream that took place in my head kept my imagination ignited and helped me make it become a reality. Also, my parents made sure my pediatrician was Black so I could witness the reality of becoming one and have someone

117

to visualize whenever someone would tell me that my dream was not realistic. My dad purchased a real stethoscope so I could feel and listen to hearts like a doctor. And what doctor would not have a science lab kit to do their own experiments in? Was it a mere coincidence that I majored in chemistry in college, or were these exposures influential? He told an eight-year-old that she would become a doctor if that's what she desired. Best of all, he implanted an entrepreneurial spirit within me and encouraged me to build my own office on the land of my late grandfather and take care of all the children of the town, empowering me with a sense of purpose. This blew my eight-year-old mind. My dreams became a vision like a scene from a Hollywood movie. If we expose our children to a variety of experiences, they get a sense of what they enjoy. During these times, we observe what gifts God has placed within them. Building confidence, supporting dreams, encouraging new adventures, and extinguishing fear are the responsibilities of parents and the adults who are privileged to work with our sons.

Encouraging an entrepreneurial spirit in your Black son can help him develop important skills such as creativity, problem-solving, and leadership. Here are some ways you can do this:

Expose them to entrepreneurship: Expose your Black son to entrepreneurship by taking them to entrepreneurial events, introducing them to successful Black entrepreneurs, and encouraging them to read books about entrepreneurship.

Encourage creativity and innovation: Encourage your Black son to think outside the box and come up with new and innovative ideas.

Allow him to explore his creativity and problem-solving skills through different activities such as brainstorming, creating prototypes, and experimenting.

Foster a growth mindset: Encourage your Black son to develop a growth mindset, where he sees challenges as opportunities to learn and grow. This can be done by praising his efforts, encouraging him to take calculated risks, and teaching him to persevere through setbacks.

Teach financial literacy: Teach your Black son about financial literacy and the basics of starting and running a business. This can include topics such as budgeting, cash flow management, and marketing.

Provide opportunities for entrepreneurship: Provide your Black son with opportunities to start his own business, such as a lemonade stand, a lawn care service, or a small online business. This can help him learn valuable skills and gain hands-on experience.

Encourage community involvement: Encourage your Black son to get involved in his community, such as volunteering or creating a project to help others. This can help him develop a sense of social responsibility and understand how entrepreneurship can positively impact his community.

Overall, encouraging an entrepreneurial spirit in your Black son requires exposing him to entrepreneurship, fostering creativity and innovation, teaching financial literacy, providing opportunities for entrepreneurship, and encouraging community involvement. By doing so, you can help him develop important skills that can lead to success in entrepreneurship and in life.

**Hugs are the new economic empowerment**

Why are hugs the new economic empowerment? Why are hugs essential? Hugs release a hormone called oxytocin, which relieves stress and enhances bonding. Boys require more hugs than girls to attain the same benefit and levels of this hormone. However, boys receive fewer hugs for many reasons. Perhaps the most common reason is the destructive myth that manliness is associated with needing less affection. Hugs are therapeutic, and ten hugs per person a day should be prescribed for the entire family. I have to admit that I have fallen short of meeting this quota, but it is never too late to start. I was raised by my father. He talked about the importance of masculinity, and his parenting technique for my brother contrasted mine. One thing he made a staple in our home was saying "I love you" to one another. My brother and I still tell one another that at the end of our phone conversations.

This leads to a very important topic: mental health. Our mental health should be considered just as vital as our physical health. Males are diagnosed less frequently with mental illness but are more likely to have their mental illnesses go unnoticed, specifically severe depression, which could end in suicide. Watch your son for any signs of internalizing, withdrawal, a lack of interest in things that used to interest him, and drug use. Therapy could be lifesaving.

It is becoming more acceptable in the Black community for people to seek mental health counseling, but unfortunately, we still have a long way to go to dispel the myth that it is taboo to release what is on your mind. The key is finding someone your son feels comfortable sharing his thoughts and concerns with. Keep the lines of communication open so that he may share any events that may erupt in his life. This will enhance counseling but not take its place because there may be things he does not feel comfortable sharing with you and would benefit by having someone neutral to discuss them with. Always remember to ask if he feels like he would like to harm himself. If he admits to feeling this way, never overlook or assume he is seeking attention. If he has a plan, has a history of suicide attempts, or admits to having attempted suicide in the past, seek emergency care immediately. Hug him and avoid judgments.

Hugs can be a powerful tool to promote the healthy development of Black boys and help to empower them economically in several ways:

- Improved Mental Health: Studies have shown that physical touch, such as hugging, can release hormones like oxytocin and reduce stress and anxiety. Regular hugs can improve a Black boy's mental health, which can help him focus better, be more productive, and make better economic decisions.

- Stronger Relationships: Hugging can strengthen relationships between family members, friends, and mentors. When Black boys feel supported and loved by those around them, they are more likely to have positive self-esteem and confidence, which can translate into success in school, work, and life.

- Increased Empathy: Hugging can also help Black boys develop empathy for others. When they receive hugs, they learn to recognize and respond to the emotional needs of others, which is an important skill in the workplace and in building healthy relationships.

- Networking: Hugging can also help Black boys build connections with others in their community. Through community events and social gatherings, they can meet new people, make new friends, and potentially even find job opportunities.

By promoting the value of hugs and encouraging more physical touch in Black boys' lives, we can help to create a culture that values their well-being, promotes their mental health, and empowers them economically. In addition to the points mentioned above, hugs can also be an effective way to promote physical health for Black boys. Hugging releases endorphins, which can help to reduce pain and improve the immune system. This can lead to fewer sick days and a higher level of productivity, which can positively impact their economic success.

Moreover, hugs can also be used as a tool for teaching emotional intelligence to Black boys. When they are hugged, they learn to recognize and understand their own emotions, which can help them better communicate and interact with others in different settings such as school, work, and social situations. Hugs can also be a way to promote self-care and self-love for Black boys. Encouraging them to hug themselves and practice self-affirmations can help them develop a positive self-image and confidence, which can be empowering in all areas of their lives, including their economic success.

Finally, hugs can be used as a tool to combat systemic racism and the trauma that Black boys may experience as a result of it. Hugs can create a safe and nurturing environment where they can feel supported and loved, which can help to reduce stress and anxiety caused by racism and discrimination. This, in turn, can lead to better mental health and greater economic empowerment.

**On the next several pages is a Checklist of suggestions for how you can promote economic empowerment with your son:**

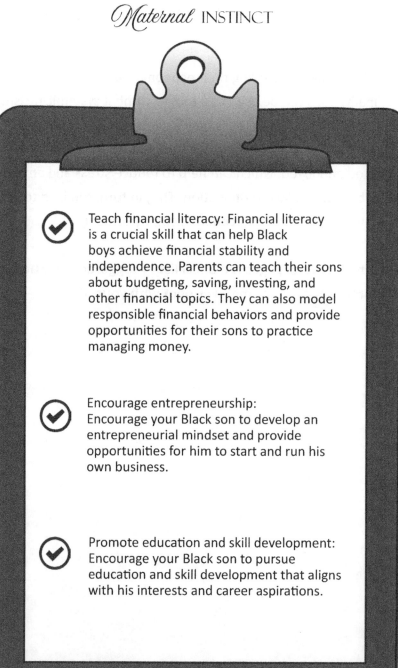

✔ Teach financial literacy: Financial literacy is a crucial skill that can help Black boys achieve financial stability and independence. Parents can teach their sons about budgeting, saving, investing, and other financial topics. They can also model responsible financial behaviors and provide opportunities for their sons to practice managing money.

✔ Encourage entrepreneurship: Encourage your Black son to develop an entrepreneurial mindset and provide opportunities for him to start and run his own business.

✔ Promote education and skill development: Encourage your Black son to pursue education and skill development that aligns with his interests and career aspirations.

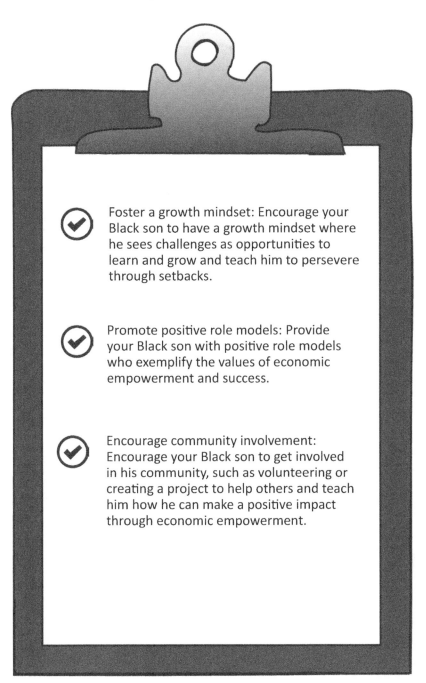

✓ Foster a growth mindset: Encourage your Black son to have a growth mindset where he sees challenges as opportunities to learn and grow and teach him to persevere through setbacks.

✓ Promote positive role models: Provide your Black son with positive role models who exemplify the values of economic empowerment and success.

✓ Encourage community involvement: Encourage your Black son to get involved in his community, such as volunteering or creating a project to help others and teach him how he can make a positive impact through economic empowerment.

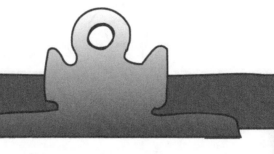

✓ Discuss financial challenges and opportunities: Discuss financial challenges and opportunities facing the Black community with your Black son to help him understand the importance of economic empowerment and the impact it can have.

✓ Encourage financial responsibility: Encourage your Black son to be financially responsible and to make informed decisions about money.

✓ Promote networking and mentorship: Encourage your Black son to build a network of mentors and professionals who can help him develop his skills and advance in his career.

✓ Provide support and encouragement: Provide your Black son with support and encouragement as he pursues economic empowerment and celebrate his successes along the way.

By following this checklist, you can help promote the ideals of economic empowerment in your sons and set them up for success in their future endeavors.

# Chapter 8

## Extracurricular Activities

*"Never underestimate the power of dreams and the influence of the human spirit. We are all the same in this notion: The potential for greatness lives within each of us."*

-Wilma Rudolph

Extracurricular activities are an important aspect of the growth and development of youth. These activities build confidence, fine and gross motor skills, hand-eye coordination, creative imagination, leadership, sportsmanship, competitive drive, logical tactics, communication skills, and even showmanship. Sports give children an opportunity to experience disappointment as well as victory in a way that mirrors reality. Participation in sports allows children to commit and dedicate time and energy to something as well as receive a feeling of self-gratification.

Athletic careers can be important to Black boys for several reasons. First, sports can provide an opportunity for Black boys to excel and achieve success in a society where they may face systemic barriers and discrimination. By excelling in sports, Black boys can gain recognition and respect, and may be able to use their athletic success as a way to open doors to other opportunities.

Additionally, sports can provide Black boys with a sense of identity and purpose. For many young Black boys, sports may be an important part of their community and cultural identity. They may feel a strong connection to the sport and to other athletes and fans, which can provide a sense of belonging and pride. Furthermore, athletic careers can provide a pathway to higher education and professional opportunities. Many colleges and universities offer athletic scholarships, which can provide a way for Black boys to access higher education that may otherwise be out of reach. In addition, a successful athletic career can lead to professional opportunities in sports or other industries, providing financial stability and career advancement.

However, it's important to note that not all Black boys are interested in or excel at sports, and that there are many other pathways to success and fulfillment. It's important to support and encourage young Black boys in whatever interests and talents they may have, rather than assuming that they should prioritize athletic success above all else.

Encouraging well-rounded goals to excel in academics, trades, as well as sports are instrumental to your son's career outcome. Always remember there is an abundance of careers where African Americans are not represented in the professional sports field. Education is a requirement for most positions, including the player. College is usually the vehicle.

**Field of dreams**

We would be kidding ourselves if we assumed that only the player gained from this relationship. Sporting organizations have survived for years because their players persistently lend their unique gifts and skills to hold the interest of spectators. The organization supplies a platform and sets up the audience; however, the player entertains the fans with a combination of athletic abilities and calculated maneuvers.

According to Gallup, American football has been the most popular sport to watch, followed by basketball and baseball. Soccer is approaching baseball in popularity. The popularity of football has decreased from 43% to 37% in 2017. This decrease has been associated with possible media and public scrutiny of domestic violence for football players, the release of the movie *Concussion*, and the silent protest of taking a knee during the pregame singing of the National Anthem by African American players in solidarity for violence and murder against African Americans by police. This movement was initiated by players such as Colin Kaepernick and Eric Reid and was highly criticized by fans and some politicians.

Parents often encourage their sons to excel at sports, hoping that they will land a job in the national sports arena. Even with the best of intentions, this plan may be too narrow. Statistics prove that only a small percentage will achieve this goal, but unfortunately, there are many statistical barriers that African American males will have to break through. As African Americans represent a higher percentage of players in the NBA and NFL, the chances of landing an administrative job such as owners, league office staff, and head coaches are 1.1% and 1.5%, respectively. The majority of administrators for the NFL are Caucasian. The NBA has a larger number of African American coaches but underrepresentation among owners and league office staff.

Rooney's Rule was created in 2003 to increase diversity among NFL coaching staff by requiring teams to interview African American candidates for head coaching and general manager positions. This rule came on the heels of the firing of two African American coaches, Tony Dungy and Dennis Green, despite their success. In 2002, Robert Johnson, BET founder, became the first African American principal owner of a professional sports team. Johnson purchased the Charlotte Bobcats and later sold the team to Michael Jordan. The NFL has yet to have an African American team owner. Reggie Fowler was a candidate to purchase the Minnesota Vikings in 2005 but did not close the deal.

**The oh-so important role of coaches**

So, what role do coaches play in this arena? The coach is there to train, develop, and direct the players individually and with a skillful craft to bring the individuals' talents together to perform as a unit. Some people coach because there is a need to fill the position. Others coach to control the fate and position of their son in a sport. This is referred to as "daddy ball" by my son and his brotherhood. Daddy ball is when a coach has a son on the team, and his position is determined by his father's preference instead of by skill and athletic ability. Most times, the other players are not afforded the opportunity to try out for the position even if they are more qualified to play that position (which is often the case). This usually happens in recreational sports because the coaches are volunteers. Club sports often incorporate a stipend for coaches in each team's budget. Club teams are usually more competitive and place stipulations on the coach-player relationship. Often, parents do not choose the coach of their son's team.

Sources indicate that certain characteristics are associated with "great" coaching. Specifically, coaches should motivate, uplift, teach, listen, observe, and lead. Coaches are human, so expect that you will find some areas that are not to your liking. They may come with their own biases and self-driven reasons for taking the job. As a parent, you must ensure that the environment is healthy for your child's development and self-esteem. Coaches should not intimidate, humiliate, or use his or her position for self-inflation. If there is a child on a team that a coach is abusing, any adults witnessing this are responsible for reporting it to the child's parent and the organization, just like in any other life situation. If an organization does not correct the actions of a coach, its integrity is not worthy of your child being an ambassador. In the end, your child is experiencing and learning behaviors that may become a part of his approach to treating others. Even worse, your child may internalize this treatment and start to dislike the sport. You will recognize a great coach most times after your child has been coached by him or her. Your personal experience with a coach may not represent the sentiments of a fellow teammate's family. Just as each coach has expectations and rewards, parents may also have their own motives.

When selecting a coach for your young Black son's team, there are several criteria that you may want to consider. Here are some potential factors to take into account:

- Experience: Look for a coach who has experience working with young athletes, particularly those in your son's age range and skill level. Consider asking about their coaching philosophy and approach to working with kids.

- Communication skills: The coach should be able to communicate effectively with both the young athletes and their parents. They should be able to explain drills and strategies in a way that is easy for kids to understand.

- Understanding of cultural diversity: It's important to choose a coach who understands and values diversity. They should be able to relate to and work well with kids from a variety of backgrounds.

- Positive attitude: Look for a coach who has a positive attitude and creates a supportive, encouraging environment for the athletes. They should be able to motivate kids to work hard and improve their skills, while also fostering a love of the game.

- Safety measures: The coach should prioritize the safety of their athletes and have appropriate measures in place to prevent injuries. They should also be trained in first aid and emergency response procedures.

- Background check: It's important to ensure that the coach has passed a background check and has no history of misconduct or abuse.

- Parent involvement: The coach should be willing to work with parents and involve them in their child's development. They should be open to feedback and willing to address any concerns or issues that arise.

- Role model: Look for a coach who serves as a positive role model for the athletes. They should be professional, respectful, and exhibit good sportsmanship.

- Inclusivity: The coach should create an inclusive environment that celebrates diversity and promotes equity. They should be committed to creating a team culture that is accepting and respectful of all athletes, regardless of their background.

- Skill development: The coach should have a focus on developing the skills of each athlete on the team, regardless of their level of ability. They should have a solid understanding of the sport and be able to provide appropriate drills and feedback to help each athlete improve.

- Flexibility: The coach should be flexible and adaptable in their coaching style, recognizing that each athlete has unique needs and learning styles. They should be able to adjust their approach to suit the needs of the individual athletes.

- Accountability: The coach should hold themselves and their athletes accountable for their actions and behavior on and off the field. They should have clear expectations and consequences for poor behavior and ensure that all athletes are treated fairly and with respect.

- Team building: The coach should promote team building and encourage athletes to work together and support each other. They should create opportunities for team bonding and emphasize the importance of teamwork.

- Feedback: The coach should provide regular feedback to athletes and parents on their progress and areas for improvement. They should be open to feedback from parents as well and use it to inform their coaching style.

Selecting a coach for your young Black son's team requires careful consideration of factors such as experience, communication skills, cultural sensitivity, safety measures, background check, parent involvement, role modeling, inclusivity, skill development, flexibility, accountability, team building, and feedback. By taking the time to find the right coach, you can help ensure that your son has a positive and rewarding experience as an athlete.

## Choosing a sports club

You have the choice to enter your son into community recreational teams or club teams. There is an array of sports for your son to try. Never assume what he will enjoy and excel in. Let him explore his options. Remember that he may say he does not enjoy a sport because of the environment or his coach's approach. In this case, try another team or organization if the first does not work out for him.

My husband and I submerged our children in introductory preschool programs that exposed them to an array of sports. As they matured, they chose the sports they enjoyed most. I suggest recreational sporting organizations to start with. Most often, they have multiple teams, and your son will feel less pressure until he determines his intensity and commitment level. Once he shows a desire to advance his skill level, club teams are an option.

On average, recreational teams may cost up to $100, which may include a uniform or T-shirt. Club teams typically run from $500 to $3500 and may not include a uniform, team gear, or equipment. The team gear can include items such as a sweatsuit, bag, and practice uniform. These itemized pieces can cost another $500. During a club season, there may be extra expenses that may not have been disclosed at the time of commitment. For example, you may have to pay for extra training, practice facilities, the coach's salary, or team mom expenses. Therefore, I recommend you get details in advance through an itemized budget and request a midseason revision. The budget is usually determined by the player fees and depends on the number of players on the roster. This can change as players withdraw or join.

Lastly, an even larger financial commitment comprises transportation expenses, food, and lodging expenses for games and tournaments. If you can find a family to carpool with, this may save you some money. Club sports prepare your son for competitive high school and college-level teams. They allow him to play against other players of a similar skill level. Club teams are often categorized into at least two or three levels.

The parents' financial and time commitments are enormous for club teams. There are ways around the time commitment, but these usually require more financial assistance. Asking relatives and close friends to assist you in both efforts would make this achievable. Instead of birthday and Christmas gifts that will sit unused, ask for help to fund your son's sports passion. If your child is older, you can hire a college student, neighbor, or car service for transportation on days that you cannot commit. Or you can start your own business with the team to fund your membership by transporting teammates to the practices and games.

Now it has not been all roses on this journey. The more competitive a club is, the higher the possibility for the practice of political and less merit-based principles, just like anything else in life. Parents have their eyes on private high schools and colleges, and some will use whatever persuasive tactics they can to achieve their goals. For some, this meat market has no boundaries. They want their son to shine because scouts may be observing.

In certain sports or clubs, African Americans are the minority, possibly due to a lack of exposure. Be prepared that these sports may not embrace your son despite his athletic ability because he may be viewed as a threat. We have attended tournaments and where there were only a handful of African American players from hundreds of teams.

Usually, the African American parents acknowledge each other with a smile and a head nod despite being from different organizations. We have encountered injustice and discrimination in organizations and with coaches. We have experienced poor coaching where a coach would rather remove a child from the field at the end of the first half after he has scored several goals to set up a win, complimenting him and not putting him back in, thereby allowing the opposing team to win. My only explanation for that is deflection or the fact that scouts might be observing, and the coach wants a specific player to shine.

In this same club, I recorded a moment prior to practice where the boys were waiting for their coach to arrive and started passing the ball to one another. My son and another young man, the only two African American players on the team, joined in. Their Caucasian teammates omitted to pass the ball to them. I could not believe what I was seeing. Their parents sat beside me on the bleachers and did not say a word to their sons, so I started recording.

This same behavior would be exhibited in games, usually causing the team to lose. During one game, the coach repeatedly yelled from the sideline for the other players to pass the ball to my son because the defenders had figured out their habit of passing to the same side and would intercept the ball every time. Finally, the player passed to my son, and the goals started coming and kept coming. These behaviors have no place in sports, and examples should be made for future life lessons.

In these frustrating situations, our approach has been professional yet direct. This may not always benefit your son, but hopefully, it will help someone else's son in the future. Remember, your responsibility of protection and advocacy is to your son. Others will witness, but do not expect them to speak out, for it is the American way. Some coaches and parents will not celebrate your son's talent or achievements, so do not expect it. That is what you are there for. That will hold true in all aspects of your son's life.

Also, recognize when you find a gem for a coach—it is life-changing and monumental for your son. My son has several coaches of whom he speaks highly and whose efforts and teachings he praises. A coach can be as influential as a father. Great coaches and teachers have a gift and realize that it is a blessing that they have the opportunity to pour it into their players and students. At least that is how I feel as a pediatrician.

The "unspoken coach's code" is my term for coaches' reactions to parents who express concerns regarding their children. The coach usually cowardly responds by punishing your child by sitting him out of the game or refusing to celebrate and encourage your son.

When your son plays for a recreational club, it is like any other business, and you are the consumer. You are not an employee who is getting paid by the organization. If you do not like what the organization is doing, you have the leverage to shop around if your son has the skills to back the move.

This is the same silent tactic that some Caucasian leaders in all arenas use to control the minority. For years, it has been handled as a myth, with videos posted on social media revealing the many racist tactics used in team sports. In the NFL, after the Colin Kaepernick movement, the owner threatened that he would not allow Kaepernick to play or get paid. Also, the NFL blocked Colin Kaepernick from acquiring a job.

This kind of institutional behavior control has been a part of American society for centuries. The privileged use their power with the right Caucasian leaders that will allow it. Even those soft, borderline Caucasian leaders who claim they are not racist are equally part of the problem. In youth sports, when coaches bully and use the "unspoken coach's code," it leaves these boys broken. Kids get it but do not process it well. They internalize, withdraw, and often quit, thinking they have done something wrong, all because adults have abused their power. Parents need to protect their children from such potential negative psychological effects. Just as parents are held to a high standard of treatment, coaches have the same level of ethics to uphold—if they do not, they must be challenged.

When parents choose a specific sports organization for their sons to join, there are a few important things to take into consideration:

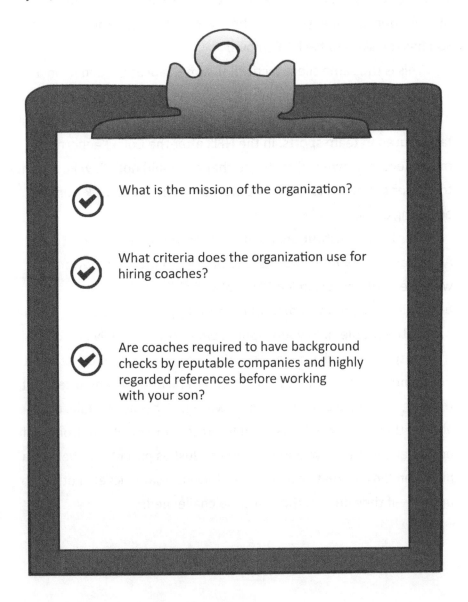

✓ What is the mission of the organization?

✓ What criteria does the organization use for hiring coaches?

✓ Are coaches required to have background checks by reputable companies and highly regarded references before working with your son?

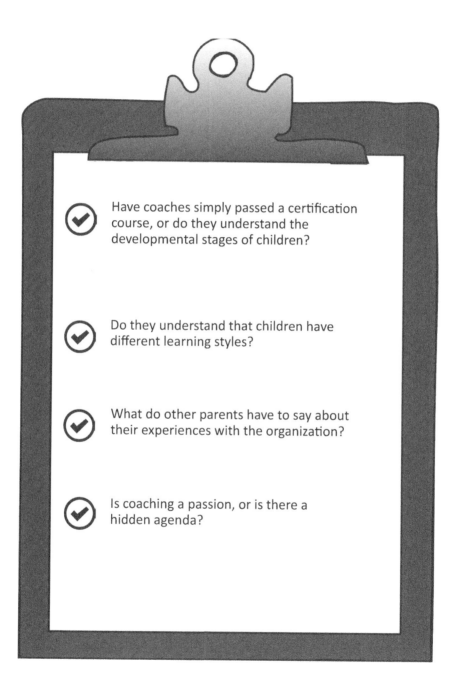

Have coaches simply passed a certification course, or do they understand the developmental stages of children?

Do they understand that children have different learning styles?

What do other parents have to say about their experiences with the organization?

Is coaching a passion, or is there a hidden agenda?

# Epilogue

*"When I dare to be powerful to use my strength in the service of my vision, then it becomes less and less important whether I am afraid."*

-Audre Lorde

**M**aternal Instinct has taken seven years to complete. On this writing journey, my son transitioned from a preteen to an adult. This is an important stage of development with abstract and logical thinking combined with impulsive risk-taking behaviors. During this time of coming into himself, entering his teen years I would have flashes back to this very phase when I recognized the transition of some of my Black male peers testing out their sophisticated thinking without a manual to their possible reckless demise. A pivotal moment in their lives where they could continue on the path to their dreams or they could falter into the devastation of crime, death, peer pressure, and not finding their way.

As time moved on, I started the book writing process with a community panel discussion just to get a feel for the temperature and what was going on in the minds of other Black people while mine was raging. This panel discussion opened up areas for mothers in the first panel discussion to express their concerns of their sons, express grief of sons murdered, and extend messages of encouragement. Professionals ranging from judges, educators, physicians, social workers, and persons from the entertainment industry participated on the panel to address questions, give advice to mothers through some of their personal experiences and their expertise since most of the panel had at least one son. After positive feedback from the panel directed to mothers, I decided to plan one for the men and lastly for the sons. It was important to get a Black male perspective of his and his peers' experience because they already walked this path. I did not need to reinvent something that was unnecessary.

So, when I began the journey of writing the book there were a few topics important to me. Education, injustice, brotherhood, extracurricular activities, financial empowerment, why boys need hugs and why they should be encouraged to cry. In the initial stage I was unsure of the approach I would take, but with processing each chapter I found myself crying. I was digging up a grave for every personal fear that left holes in my soul dating back to college when I began to process the unique trajectory of Black males. Through the process of writing, I started putting the dirt back in the ground. This book was therapeutic in so many ways. You see I am a pediatrician by profession, but a Black mother chosen by God for this task of raising a Black son. I have been afforded the chance to speak with children, especially teenagers, about their goals in life and what makes them happy. I talk to them as if it is my last opportunity. And when I get in the room with Black boys, I see my son. I often see concern in his mother's eyes of wanting to know what is it that can be done to assure his safety and success. Boys know their mothers will be there no matter what. My professional experience confirms that Black boys are no different than boys of other races. They may just have a different swag. The innocence, the love, the intent, the vibrance they have for life is mirrored. Sometimes speaking with these boys helps me to process my thoughts with my own son. I am often disgusted with continuous playbacks of negative imagery from media and news outlets. Is this truly a representation of you? The murders we all have watched over and over again. The hunting of Black men, boys and women by those who took an oath similar to my medical Hippocratic oath; however, for some public servants it is hypocritical. Both are meant to uphold ethical morals to serve and protect citizens. How does this happen? And when will this happen to your child? So we teach, we preach, and we pray every day but the killings just keep on coming. Even in our own communities, the value of life is not processed before senseless shootings. I grew up in Baltimore and I have watched this mindset transform through the eras. How do we stop this? How do we teach love? To love our brothers and sisters, we first must understand the first love which is God's love. We have to second understand and embrace self-love because if we value our own lives we may not choose to take someone else's life so quickly.

Education has been top on my list. Without a solid educational foundation in this society there can be some areas of restricted access. My vision is for every Black boy to be granted the opportunity of a full day of pre-kindergarten age three and prekindergarten age four before entering kindergarten with his peers. This opportunity will close the gap in disparity and decrease his disciplinary time out of the classroom. The ultimate goal is to decrease the number of Black boys sentenced to private prison institutions and appropriate funds for the educational system for teachers, schools, supplies and technology.

I always attempted to assure that my children were in the best education environments that I could afford at the time. And there are excellent educational opportunities in all sectors, but you have to do your research. You have to plan your life around these opportunities if it means moving across town to be in a certain zone. Redlining is not extinct. Speaking to teachers and your superintendents, going to meetings, serving on the Parent Teacher Association (PTA), knowing the principal and vice principal by first name not because he is in trouble but because you have that right are key. Visiting the school just to see how his day is going. Setting high expectations individually for each child. You never allow anyone to lower your standards because you know your child best.

Mothers, begin to develop your mommy pod list. This list should consist of at least five people you consider trustworthy enough to step into your place when you need assistance. The people in this pod may range in ages, gender, but it must be someone you can entrust your child's life with, protect morals you have set, and not undermine your values. This will help or assist you when you have an emergency or when you just can't make it in time. You are running late from work to the school, and you need someone to cover you for ten minutes at the end of after care. Spend time on this list. This list is not permanent because life happens for people, and they may no longer be available to commit. But it is so important that we go back to that village mentality and show our kids they have other adults too that they can lean toward if needed. Also with Maternal Instinct, each mom should identify with two mother mentors and at least two potential mother mentees. The goal is for generations of mothers to share and learn through witness and communication amongst each other.

Healthy brotherhood and activity is so important for boys. Your son's brotherhood and their trajectory oftentimes may determine the path they take. Exposing your children to arts, sports, and things outside your family life may stimulate them in a positive way. Maybe switch up your routine for example instead of the trampoline park, go to a community theater production or vice versa. Make a list of your son's brotherhood, another of your child's activities, and another of activities you aspire to do in the future.

Moms also if you can find three strong Black male role models who are present in your son's life. These Black men while preferred may not be constant in his life but more importantly your son is aware of the positive contributions to life that these men have made to be role modeled. As mothers we have our own contributions of showing our sons how to love but boys need to see how men move in situations, how they build, how they protect, how they make opportunities, and become strong leaders in their home, communities, and their jobs. They need to witness this example for appropriate behavior development.

Now that my son is twenty, I am at another stage of concern. The fear that was cultivated when the lives of Sadiq Martin, Kenneth Bowman, and Bruce Hamilton were snatched. This is the age and stage of maturity where late adolescents and young adults are acting out the acceptance of the baton to think and make decisions without adult guidance. My son is now entering his third year of college. Living on his own in a big city, experiencing life for himself, and making decisions without me or his dad. Some may ask why I fear since he is on his own path to life. He is majoring in electrical engineering, and you have carried this fear all his life. Yes, this is the same child that would challenge himself to reciting the alphabet with sounds as fast as he could for kicks by three years old. He would sit with the adult males at the family functions, weddings, or whatever setting, find the men and could carry a conversation about the statistics of football, basketball and many other sports and name who was going to be the best seed at a very young age. But this too was the child at three years old as we rode through Baltimore city while sitting in his car seat would peer out the window and turn to me and say, "mom I want stripes (braids) in my hair" and while he was still in a diaper, he would mimic trying to wear his pants below his diaper. I could not understand because there was no one in the home or in his environment who was doing that. But I could see he was watching everything and everyone. And yet I could not protect him against everyone and everything. And by the way he finally got those braids a few months ago and he had the biggest smile when he took off the doo rag to show me. All this to say is they are going to make their own path and their own decisions. We are here as a guide as they experience growing pains.

I know that mothers of Black sons and many others are going to unify for the overall restoration of Black boys in America. The results of this movement of moms and allies is going to be life changing for every Black male ever born. There will be no affinity for aid based on his social economics, cultural heritage, or ability. The conversations that we begin to openly discuss will no longer shelter and bury trauma experiences but will open up minds and bring positive results. And some may ask why are you so focused on Black boys. And my answer to that is we have to go back to building strong foundations for our families. And although families have been broken down and destroyed, we have an opportunity to rebuild because no one else is going to do this for us. It would be practical to start with Black boys since the design has been to silence his existence. Yes women, we are making strides. We are supporting ourselves and families but we have to bring awareness to the potential demise of our Black boys so they transition into Black men who can carry generations forward. And if we don't their numbers will continue to dwindle. Not on my watch and not on a Black mother's watch. I challenge all, even those who do not have Black sons. There is a Black boy somewhere and you can join his mommy pod. I Challenge you to join the movement. Let's bring love back to our families, our communities, and our sons.

# Sentiments
## From My Brothers

*"A good head and a good heart are always a formidable combination."*

-Nelson Mandela

# *Maternal* INSTINCT

Hello, my name is Daniel T. Nicholson, IV, more affectionately known as Ooey, and I am a retired Baltimore Police Department Homicide Detective and current Campus Investigator/Detective at Lincoln University in Pennsylvania. I met Dr. Stacey Eadie in middle school at Roland Park Middle in 1983. As a bright, fun-loving, and even back then, socially conscious young lady, I knew that my friend, Stacey, was going to do great things in this world. We both were raised in the inner city of Baltimore and attended public schools. However, we both were raised to have genuine respect not only for ourselves, but for those around us.

In today's society, we're always blaming the school system for our children's lack of good grades when in fact we should be blaming ourselves...THE PARENTS. Lord knows if I, or Stacey, had taken any unsatisfactory grades home to our parents then all "you know what" would break loose. Meaning, our parents would kill us. My mother, Gloria Whittington, raised my brother and I basically all on her own. We didn't have the latest and greatest however, we were blessed with EVERYTHING we needed and most of what we wanted. We were showered with love and disciplined when we stepped out of line. We were not spoiled, as the Bible would say, because my mother did not spare the rod! And to this very day, my brother and I are successful men with beautiful families of our own. And I have my mother to thank for it.

As I close, I remember a time in 7th grade, Stacey and I were in Mr. Gall's algebra class, and she was having a bit of difficulty. She turned to me and asked for help. And being the friend that I am, I gave it to her and she has gone on to getting her Doctorate! She knew way back then that there was no way possible she was taking home any unsatisfactory grades because that would surely result in some type of punishment and/or forfeiture of some type of fun or entertainment... even if it only meant she could not rock her Georgetown Starter jacket to school with her pinstriped Lees and shellhead Adidas. Oh, my sister was FLY! BELIEVE THAT! I'm proud of her and I'm even more proud to be considered her friend/brother since 1983. I love you, Stacey.

**Daniel T. Nicholson, IV**
**Retired Law Enforcement**

*I would like to congratulate my sista (Dr. Eadie) for all the accomplishments she has gathered as a strong and professional woman in the field of medicine. Also, I would like to extend a major salute for her inspiring work within the larger community in the Maryland area. Words cannot describe the elation I have for my sista (Dr. Eadie). I have known Dr. Eadie since elementary school. We both attended Howard Park ES and Calvin Rodwell ES in Baltimore, MD respectively. Dr. Eadie and my sister (Dr. Sayyida Abdus-Salaam) are best friends. They have been best friends since first grade. They are both remarkable and incredible women. They have a bond that is unbreakable, and I remember they made a pact to become doctors since middle school (Roland Park MS). They both share a love for medicine, enhancing the community through various outreach programs, assisting all people in need, and New Edition. Yes, Ronnie, Bobby, Ricky, Mike, and Ralph. Ralph is Dr. Eadie's favorite. The leader of the band. I share this to illustrate how this book is important to Black males in America. Black Men are natural born leaders, however, as a Black Man we have endured PAIN on many levels since the diaspora and beyond. I know as a Black Man, we are judged very harshly and very often the light that shines on Black Men is bleak at the center stage. New Edition as a group exemplifies strength and ONENESS. They move and sing as ONE entity. We as Black Men need to come together and work as ONE to overcome the PAIN. I believe this book will showcase the strengths, talents, triumphs and negatives associated within our communities throughout the U.S.*

*WHY is this book important? Sadiq Ali Martin, my little brother was murdered in 1991 in Baltimore by a police officer. It was police brutality. The pain rocked our community in West Baltimore, where Dr. Eadie and I were raised. We had some great experiences as kids in West Baltimore. However, in September of 1991, a dark cloud hovered over us and changed our lives forever. I cannot change the circumstance that occurred with my brother; however, I can continue to reach out and create change within our community through education and awareness. At the time of my brother's death, I was a student at Howard University. I wanted to give up because the core of my spirit was rocked. The world continued to turn, and I was lost. The killing of Black Men has to stop. My mother, Shawishi Martin is a true QUEEN and survivor. The message she would share with my brother* and I daily before going to school or enjoying our lives within the neighborhood with friends was "GOD is GREAT!" She would always say "You are always in GOD's mighty hands" and fear nothing. She raised warriors and leaders. I know I'm a leader and warrior within this physical world and my brother is a leader in the spiritual world. He is with GOD and all the brothers who transcended and perished are forever in his hands. Thank you Dr. Eadie for everything you do and my hope this book inspires peace, love, and prosperity among all people. Pain can become LOVE and love can become PAIN; however, we don't have to move as a hurt people. We must move with LOVE and my hope this book fills your heart with beautiful energy. God Bless.

**Ma'ani Martin**
**Brother from Another Mother**

Congratulations on the book. You are truly inspirational. Mothering a young Black male is challenging and exciting. There are things we want to ask our mom but feel we can't. Dr Eadie has shown that these delicate but important matters can be addressed by a son and his mom. It has been a treasure to see her raise such a gentleman.

**Dr. William Dash**
**Pediatric Concierge and Study Buddy**

Stacey,
Congratulations on the completion of your First book, Maternal Instinct. Your commitment to building and growing healthy families physically, mentally, and spiritually should be applauded. These days we need support and guidance in keeping our communities from falling apart and too many times ending in heartbreak and tragedy. Your book is an outline on how we could avoid those outcomes. Your experiences and observations, concerning young Black Men, shows your compassion and love for their well-being. Once again, CONGRATULATIONS, and I'm SO PROUD of you. I love you!

**Howard Brian Eadie**
**Big Brother**

*This message is with sincere congratulations for Dr. Stacey Eadie. I have known Stacey for 34 years starting when we first met during her 1989 Summer Laser Training at Lincoln University. We have been friends ever since that point. We've helped each other in various areas of our lives these past 34 years and I'm very much proud of all that Stacey has accomplished. This book is just another example of Stacey making an impact for and in this world.*

*I'm currently a Collective Bargaining Specialist for the National Education Association, a teacher's union. I'm also humbly Blessed to be the Pastor of Understanding the Bible Ambassadors' Assembly, located in Clayton, Delaware. I've been married to my wife, Jamie, for 25 years, and we have two children/young adults, my son Malon and my daughter Adiah. My entire life, my mom, Gwen Lassiter, has been a Blessing in my life. Her unconditional love, including, but not limited to her support, encouragement, guidance, wisdom, and correction have indeed helped shape me. I love her immensely!!! GOD has a distinct and unique purpose for the mother's role in helping to raise male children....the part that a mother fulfills is invaluable in the rearing of a male child.*

**Mike Holmes**
**Lincoln University Big Brother**

*As a child I was told by my mom that I couldn't go to a friend's house until she met their parents or if I was outside playing, I had to go in when the streetlights came on. When I got older, I was instructed to call home when I got to my destination. That was back in the day when your parents knew your every move and people in the community knew your family.*

*Today, the challenges of raising children, especially sons, are much more difficult. To make matters worse is that most children are being raised in a single parent household where the mother is the head of the house. Some of the fears/concerns that these mothers have range from the substandard education that their sons are receiving in the underfunded schools to the violence that lies outside of the doors in which they live to the racial injustices they face because of the color of their skin.*

Kudos to Dr. Stacey Eadie for tackling these matters and more. Bringing these matters to light in this book is brilliant and insightful. Being a pediatrician, her vantage point is different because she interacts with the mothers of these boys from a different angle. It's time for us men in the community to take back our position and help right this sinking ship.

I am very proud of Dr Eadie on so many levels, but this book is the icing on the cake. I have been fortunate to see her journey begin as an undergraduate at Lincoln University as well as doing a rotation in my City of Philadelphia. Stacey is a great example of a woman, mother, wife and medical professional. Because of this I would like to say congratulations on the book and thank you for being a friend.

**Michael Bailey**
**Lincoln University. Entreprenuer, and Big Brother**

First of all, I am extremely proud of your accomplishments Stacey and what you have done for the Community. Dr. Eadie and I met during our Pediatric residency at Wayne State University/Children's Hospital of Michigan. I even had the pleasure of being one of your guests on your podcast discussing COVID19. My mother told me to read Proverbs chapter 3 in its entirety at least once a year. The entire chapter is a narrative of biblical Wisdom to a son. The opening sentence of Proverbs 3 "My Son, do not forget my teaching" has always comforted me. I am currently practicing Internal Medicine/ Pediatrics at Baptist Health Hospital in Lexington Kentucky.

Blessing to you Dr. Eadie in these next chapters

**Jai Gilliam, M.D.**
**Pediatric Residency Brother**

I take great pleasure and am honored to share my sentiments with Dr. Stacey Eadie for such a needed and timely work of heart, Maternal Instinct. I had the privilege of knowing Dr. Eadie while we were young, undergrad STEM students at Lincoln University, PA through an intensive summer STEM program that was a requirement before freshman year. I am proud to call her a friend and a fellow alum and am excited that she is an author.

*I was 12 years old when my parents divorced and have firsthand experience of being raised by a single mom. It was my mother's unconditional love, sacrifice, discipline and guidance that kept me from being another statistic as a Black boy raised in West Philadelphia. She and my grandparents ensured I had the best education and exposed me to extra-curricular activities such as playing piano, riding horses and learning archery every summer at overnight YMCA summer camp, participating in chess club, joining after-school reading programs at the local library, and playing sports. She also kept me involved in church. All these activities coupled with doing chores before going outside to play with my friends and earning/spending money shaped me into the family man I've become. My education led me to an engineering career that began at NASA and has continued for the past 25 years as a technical sales consultant at AT&T. I would not be where I am without my mother and grandmother who raised the standard and would not let me settle beneath my potential. It is not through my own efforts that got me where I am, but it is because of their prayers, time, investment, Godly example, and their nurturing, but strong, tough love. I want to encourage all readers to make a commitment to invest and to impart love, wisdom, grace, identity, opportunity, and exposure into the lives of the next generation so that they can maximize every opportunity to fulfill their dreams and live life to their fullest potential. It is hard work, it is heart work, but let's do it, because it is worth the work. I'm living proof! Thank you and continued blessings to you and your beautiful family Dr. Stacey Eadie!*

**Michael Canty**
**Lincoln University LASER Big Brother**

*I have known my wife, Dr Stacey Eadie, for over thirty years. We met in front of her dorm which sat in the center of the campus of Lincoln University in Pennsylvania during my freshman year. It was a bright and sunny day and as I remember, Stacey in an intentional, conservative and witty yet flirtatious tone caught my attention with conversation. From that moment we became friends for seven years before we would return to the 1998 Lincoln University homecoming where we exchanged phone numbers, and our life story began.*

My impression of the young twenty-year-old Stacey was that she was cute and funny. As a mature woman, I recognize that my earlier impressions were true but there was much more I could not see then. My wife is loving, dependable, tolerant, focused and a multitasker. Throughout our marriage I have watched her care for her patients and come home to the demands of our children and myself all with that smile you see on the back cover of this book. If you are a family member or a friend, she will do whatever is needed. Like my mother, she is caring. And I just love her for who she is.

I have learned a lot watching her plan out our children's educational paths and activities and I support her in any way possible. We complement each other well because instead, finances are my strong suit.

During the COVID-19 pandemic she played many roles that demanded her to leave the comfort and safety of our home in which I had no intentions of leaving. She made protocols to keep everyone she was responsible for safe like her family, her stepmom whom she is caregiver for, her staff, and every patient especially the newborns. And we all remained healthy.

My mother had three boys. She would worry whenever we stepped out the door, but she knew she raised us to have integrity. I lived to see her smile that lit up a room whenever I came to town to visit.

Congratulations Stacey for becoming a first time author. I commend you for stepping into new territories to offer yourself to the community. Lives will be blessed. Your parents are pleased.

**Phene Jean-Claude,**
**Your husband**

# Acknowledgments

*"My humanity is bound up in yours, for we can only be human together."*

-Desmond Tutu

To the most high God, I humbly come before you to thank you first for granting me life when the statistics of medicine counted me out for survival of my birth defect declaring it a miracle. For your unfailing faithfulness that has brought me through every adversity. You stripped me of every dependency to enhance my acuity of your presence in my life. What is faith without tests? Use me Lord. Teach me to walk in your light. Choose my words for your work. Let us begin this journey of healing and remodeling.

Sincerest gratitude to my husband who supported my writing this book until he would read the detailed intimacy of the conception of our first child in black and white. I love you. Thank you for supporting my ventures and allowing me to be me. You are my Rock.

To my talented children, Phene and Xay, you mean the world to me. I thank God for choosing me to parent you. Watching His gifts manifest in your life is priceless. Both of you lead, create, influence, catalyze and exemplify God's brilliance and love.

To Dap Daddy in heaven, your sacrifice, wisdom, unconditional love, paternal instinct, strength, intuition are your superpowers. You set the bar for life fulfillment. I pray I am still making you proud. Your one and only Princess.

Roses to my late mother, prototype, spiritual guide whose life was taken way too soon. May your soul rest from worrying about all the things you could not pass on due to your premature death. The serenity of the unspoken conversations are in messages you left on the back of pictures for me to read later.

To my big brother, Howard Eadie, for being my first best friend and protector. You can never say enough times of how proud you are of me to remind me of daddy. Those words keep me pressing. You are my hero.

To my stepmother, Carolyn Conner, for always treating me as your own and accepting the torch my father requested before passing. Your teachings of womanhood and ambassador of the teachings of Christ are just a portion of your character. I will never forget you confiscating my Prince Purple Rain cassette at eleven years of age after witnessing me sing the lyrics Darling Nicky "masturbating with a magazine". I can still hear the loud click of the eject button followed by the plastic cassette hitting the door of my boom box. After a loving dictionary definition and bible scripture on masturbating, not only did I learn a new word, but I understood there were consequences for my actions.

My nieces, great niece, cousins, aunts, and uncles for loving and supporting me. To my two older cousins Charles Rudolph Rochester, Jr. and Dr. Reginald Eadie your genius, ambition and drive not only has served as my example but as a blueprint for my son as well. You are held in his highest regards.

"Most valuable player" awarded to Dr. Larthenia Howard, my brilliant book coach and sorority sister. Your masterful mind, relentless dedication and belief to this project coupled with your perfected, creative craft enhanced the birthing process of *Maternal Instinct*. Over the years I have been blessed to experience your detailed assignments turn into masterpieces.

To the Black males in my life, you are the inspiration for needing to write this book. Know that you are rare and precious as black diamonds. All the Black males through my twenty-six-year educational experience, elementary through medical school and residency training who represent the iron that Proverbs refers to, that continuously sharpened my iron. Thank you for your presence, competition, support, motivation, protection and genuine love.

A special tribute to Sadiq Ali Martin, Kenneth Blake Bowman, and Bruce Hamilton. My memories of you will forever be stamped on my heart. Each of your lives were taken within a year of entering manhood and graduating high school. You represent the pain and trauma of my experience and reason I will not stop. I will not let your spirits be forgotten. If only your murderers knew what your vibrant smiles meant to me and your loved ones.

To my Synergy Sisters Dr. Sayyida Martin, Blanche Turner, Dr. Lernice Henry, Nicole Holland, Dr. Cynthia Penn, Dr. Michele Reed, Dr. Andrea Goings, Jamie Holmes, Dr. Robin Moore, Dr. Jonnie Robinson, Dr. Michelle Davis-Dash, Stacey Williams, Tori Soudan, Afriqiyah Woods, Deborah Blakely, Hope Lights, Quibulah Graham, and Danielle Giddins, I love you. Thank you for your continuous support, encouragement, and sisterhood.

Power and light to my spiritual whisperers, Carolyn Byrd (prophet), Dr. Jeri Dyson (warrior), and Tylis Cooper (body and mind trainer). You are vessels that transmit directed messages from God himself. Light received.

A few special gems to bestselling authors Zane, LaJoyce Brookshire, and Candace Sandy for the conception and mental massaging of my first book, *Maternal Instinct* at the Writer's Boot Camp in March of 2016.

For all the participants and guests of the Maternal Instinct panel series in the fall of 2016 for mothers, men, and sons. To name a few - Honorable Wanda Heard, Wanda Durant "The Real MVP", Dr. Jeri Dyson (moderator), Dr. Carols Williams, Derrick Chase, Vickie Bowman, Dr. Ocheze Joseph, Rosemary Anderson, Phene Jean-Claude, Howard Brian Eadie, Eric C. Webb, Marvin McKenstry Jr.,

# ACKNOWLEDGMENTS

Nadir Nasheed, Tim Gordon, Jeffrey Wright, Dr. Christian Anderson, Matthew Prestbury, Tony Roberts, Stanley Harper, Dr. Ashanti Woods, Dr. William Dash, Bobby Marvin Holmes and guests. Thank you for seeing the vision before I put the pen to paper. Those initial discussions set a golden foundation for the chapters.

Forever grateful for the angel, Charmaine West, videography and photography for her creative work and capturing the moments of the panel discussion. To the Holmes family for your loving touches during the panel discussion.

To the brotherhood mother tribe, Donna, Latasha, Alika, Jami, Christina, Rosemary, Ginna, LaTonia, and Karen for the bonds forged through the love of our sons. Thank you for the open home policy, pick up or drop off and serving as surrogate mother when my children were in your presence. I cannot thank you without thanking the dads, Phene, Osbourne, Howard, Chris, and Troy for coaching recreational basketball and or serving as role models for not only our boys but those teammates who did not have a father figure present in their lives.

To the educational administrators and teachers, especially Timera Loftin and Tonya Brogden for recognizing our son's gifts and talents at an early age and giving your honest advice for recommendations for schools. You understood the pure nature of Black boys and poured love into them in prekindergarten and kindergarten that exist until this day as memories of his favorite teachers. Expressions that confirmed that our boys had a safe space to go to instead of punishment as a solution.

To my patients' mothers I appreciate you entrusting me with the medical care of your children along with allowing yourself to be vulnerable enough to share your individual concerns with raising your Black son in this still racist society.

To those who oppose the views of this book, thank you for purchasing *Maternal Instinct*. Possibly after reading, you will collaborate for the injustice of Black males. Ask yourself, would you give up all your privilege and trade places with him.

# About Dr. Stacey Eadie

*"If you are going to achieve excellence in big things, you develop the habit in little matters. Excellence is not an exception; it is a prevailing attitude."*

-Colin Powell

For over twenty-one years Dr. Stacey Eadie, a Board-Certified Pediatrician, through her unique art of medicine enhances the health of children from birth to age 21 through listening, treating, and empowering parents on preventative methods for healthy lifestyles. In her determination to create her vision for the experience of her patient's families, twelve years ago she established her own practice, Peds In A Pod Pediatrics, LLC in her hometown of Baltimore. Dr. Eadie offers her gifts and talents to adolescents and young adults outside of the office through voluntary mentorship programs such as those she founded (Soul Sisters and Underground Pipeline to Medicine), through her alma mater and first historically Black college and university, Lincoln University's career series and student organized panel series, and church and sorority youth leadership programs.

To fulfill her passion of education, Dr. Eadie finds pleasure in serving on a career and technical education advisory council in her

167

county. During the COVID-19 global pandemic quarantine, Dr. Eadie found gratification in participating in virtual programs such as a youth medical mentor program for Disney, conversations with the mayor of New Jersey on COVID-19 vaccine confidence, engaging in medical topics with Doni Glover's Bmorenews.com, creating and executing Baby Docs a social media Live interactive educational series. Dr. Eadie cohosted Baby Docs with her colleague to give a lifeline to the community on health questions during a dark time. Later, she shared her honest expertise in the COVID vaccination townhall sponsored by the National Council of Negro Women (92 Q, 95.9 FM, Radio One). She received the Bmorenews.com's Joe Manns Black Wall Street Honoree Award, alongside so many of those she held in high esteem growing up in Baltimore. For over half her life, Dr. Eadie has been a member of Alpha Kappa Alpha Sorority, Incorporated and recognized as a Silver Star and Charter Member of the Alpha Beta Gamma Omega Chapter.

Most cherished, Dr. Eadie holds her husband and two children in highest regard, recognizing and appreciating the foundation of the enrichment of their support and love.

Made in the USA
Middletown, DE
21 October 2023

41201993R00099